PADDLE
THE EAST OF ENGLAND

The Best Places to Go with a Paddleboard, Kayak or Canoe

ADLARD COLES
Bloomsbury Publishing Plc
50 Bedford Square, London, WC1B 3DP, UK
29 Earlsfort Terrace, Dublin 2, Ireland

BLOOMSBURY, ADLARD COLES and the
Adlard Coles logo are trademarks of
Bloomsbury Publishing Plc

First published in Great Britain 2025

Copyright © Jess Ashley, Oli Jordan, Andy Large and Matt Payne

Jess Ashley, Oli Jordan, Andy Large and Matt Payne have asserted their right under the Copyright, Designs and Patents Act, 1988, to be identified as Authors of this work

All rights reserved. No part of this publication may be: i) reproduced or transmitted in any form, electronic or mechanical, including photocopying, recording or by means of any information storage or retrieval system without prior permission in writing from the publishers; or ii) used or reproduced in any way for the training, development or operation of artificial intelligence (AI) technologies, including generative AI technologies. The rights holders expressly reserve this publication from the text and data mining exception as per Article 4(3) of the Digital Single Market Directive (EU) 2019/790

A catalogue record for this book is available from the British Library

ISBN: PB: 978-1-3994-1843-0; eBook: 978-1-3994-1845-4; e-PDF: 978-1-3994-1844-7

2 4 6 8 10 9 7 5 3 1

Art Editor Louise Turpin, Typeset in Frutiger Condensed
Printed and bound in India by Replika Press Pvt. Ltd.

To find out more about our authors and books visit www.bloomsbury.com and sign up for our newsletters

IMPORTANT SAFETY NOTICE AND LEGAL DISCLAIMER

This book contains descriptions of paddling routes and locations around the UK. Undertaking any activity on or near water carries with it some risks that cannot be entirely eliminated, for example, you might get lost on a route or caught in bad weather. The information contained in this book should not be relied upon as a sole means of navigation. Users should consult all other relevant and available publications and information, such as the local Harbour Authority guidance or Waterway Authorities Navigation Notices. Users should also check local weather and water conditions with the appropriate authorities prior to departure.

The guidance contained in this book is based on the accumulated experience of the authors. Such guidance is generic and takes no account of users' own experience, advice from other paddlers, actual or forecast meteorological conditions, water conditions or other waterway users powered or otherwise.

All internet addresses given in this book were correct at the time of going to press. Bloomsbury Publishing Plc does not have any control over, or responsibility for, any third-party websites referred to or in this book.

The publishers and authors accept no responsibility for any errors or omissions, or for any accident, loss or damage arising from the misuse of information or guidance contained in this book.

PADDLE
THE EAST OF ENGLAND

The Best Places to Go with a
Paddleboard, Kayak or Canoe

Jess Ashley, Oli Jordan,
Andy Large and Matt Payne

ADLARD COLES

LONDON · OXFORD · NEW YORK · NEW DELHI · SYDNEY

CONTENTS

Introduction	6
What to wear	6
What to take	10
Guide to safety	10
Licences	12

ESSEX

1	Brightlingsea to Wivenhoe	16
2	Chelmer and Blackwater Navigation	21
3	Dovercourt Bay	26
4	Brightlingsea Estuary and the Creeks	30
5	Sawbridgeworth to Harlow	36
6	Dedham to Flatford	41
7	River Colne	45
8	Osea Island	50
9	Two Tree Island to Mulberry Harbour	53
10	Mersea Island to Tollesbury	57
11	Maldon Loop	62
12	Mulberry Harbour and Southend Pier	67
13	Mersea Island to the Strood	71
14	Mersea Island Circumnavigation	76

SUFFOLK

15	Waldringfield	84
16	Sudbury to the Henny Swan	90
17	Pin Mill to Orwell Bridge	93
18	Bures to Lamarsh	98
19	Nayland to Wissington Weir	102
20	Stratford St Mary to the Langham Flumes	108

NORFOLK

21 Coltishall to Buxton Mill	118
22 Rockland Broad and The Slaughters	122
23 Norwich City Paddle	126
24 Surlingham Broad and Bargate	134
25 Bungay Loop	140

CAMBRIDGESHIRE

26 Ely – River Great Ouse	146
27 Cambridge – The Backs	152

BEDFORDSHIRE

28 Kempston to Bedford Town Centre & Top River	162
29 Cardington to Bedford Town Centre	168
30 Great Barford to Willington Lock	172

HERTFORDSHIRE

31 Bishop's Stortford to Twyford Mill Lock	180

Picture credits	186
Index	190
Acknowledgements	192

INTRODUCTION

Join us and experience the wonders that we have available in the East of England!

The East of England coastline is a paddler's paradise. Whether you're a seasoned kayaker or a curious paddleboard enthusiast, the calm waters, scenic rivers and charming villages offer something for everyone. Explore historic waterways, spot wildlife in nature reserves, or simply relax on a peaceful paddle with stunning scenery all around. From shorter, playful paddles to full-day paddles, *Paddle The East of England* is a great place to explore!

This book will cover some of the most popular paddle sites across:
- Essex
- Suffolk
- Norfolk
- Cambridgeshire
- Bedfordshire
- Hertfordshire

BELOW Beautiful sunrise paddle at Alresford Creek.

Featuring beautiful photography and clear maps, this is the essential guide to exploring the East of England's most popular waterways.

What to wear

This is a simple guide with some options that we at East of England Paddlesports (EOEPS) have used over the years. This isn't a set of rules – we're not saying what you have to wear, and everybody is different – but the best advice is to dress for the water, and the weather. It might be quite a mild, sunny winter's day, but the water could be really, really cold, and cold water shock is always a risk. Also, bear in mind that normal clothing (jeans, hoodies, etc) retains a lot of water and can be very heavy when soaked.

It is also worth considering taking a change of clothes, or extra layers in a dry bag, in case you get wet or the weather changes. Layers also help, as you can add or remove them as the weather/temperature changes.

We have separated this guidance into five main areas: base layers, top layers, wetsuits, drysuits, and head, hands and feet.

Base layers Base layers are very flexible and can be worn by themselves, as a layer under clothing, such as wet and drysuits, or as additional layers. They don't have to be watersport specific; a lot of generic active wear will be suitable. The key is to make sure it fits well, has good wicking qualities and is fit for purpose, for example it won't cause additional risks of snagging or entrapment.

Watersports rash vests and leggings are perfect as they are usually made from thin, silky material and designed for this use. They also come in thermal styles as well, for additional warmth. Worn under a wetsuit, they can help to reduce chaffing and make it easier to get the wetsuit on.

Top layers A good water/windproof layer is essential, even stowed in the dry bag in case the weather changes. Avoid fleece-lined items (unless specifically designed for watersports), as they will hold a lot of water and get heavy when wet.

For your upper body, a simple waterproof top, like a sailing cagoule, is a good value option, but lots of kayaking and Stand up Paddleboarding (SUP) clothing specialists also offer great tops with good features designed specifically for the type of paddling you'll be doing. Dry cags for kayaking in a sit-in kayak help keep you totally dry, with only your head and hands exposed. Lots of pockets and drawstrings should be avoided, as they can cause entrapment issues or make self-rescue harder.

There are a lot of options for legs, from chest-high waterproof trousers to trousers with built-in feet, but again, do make sure they are fit for purpose. Built-in feet once submerged can fill with water, making self-rescue very difficult.

Wetsuits The first point to mention about wetsuits is that they are designed to be in the water, which is where they work best.

ABOVE Rash vest and shorts (pumping board).

Neoprene has tiny bubbles in it and when dry, insulates you and keeps you warm. When in the water, the fabric traps small layers of water next to your skin, which your body warms up, and you stay warmer than without the wetsuit. That water evaporates when a wet wetsuit is exposed to wind, and the wearer can seem colder for a while. As always, there is a balance between risk and reward.

Having said that, a wetsuit is a great option for many paddlers and they come in a lot of different sizes, styles and thicknesses, some being semi-dry.

Shortie wetsuits are exactly that – they have short arms and legs. A Long John/Jane has long legs, a vest-style top and usually zips up the front. These are great for paddling as they allow for more movement around the shoulders. Full wetsuits have full coverage and can zip up the front, back or across the chest. You can also get wetsuit leggings and separate tops (like a jumper) to really mix and match layers and options.

Summer wetsuits are typically 1–3mm thick, while winter wetsuits are around

ABOVE Andy in his U-Zip drysuit.
TOP RIGHT Oli in his leg-entry drysuit.
RIGHT Chest entry and Long John wetsuit.

5mm and above and can have titanium or fleecy linings for added warmth.

Most important is the fit. To work properly, wetsuits have to be snug, although you may want to add base layers underneath, so try a few on for the best fit.

Prices vary and generally the more you spend the better the neoprene will be in terms of flexibility and performance.

Drysuits
Drysuits are exactly that: suits to keep you dry. However, you can still feel the water/weather temperatures through them, so good, high-wicking base/under layers are essential to keep you warm.

Drysuits can be seen as expensive items but they are very versatile and can be used in many different conditions. They range from basic all-round suits to suits designed specifically for the type of paddling being undertaken, so they have various openings at the rear, front, U-shaped, middle and two-piece. Neck and wrist seals require good care and maintenance to ensure long life.

Head, hands and feet
We often have paddlers asking us how to keep their hands and feet warm, although equally (in the case of paddleboarding) some prefer to feel the board with bare feet. As with all things, it's down to personal preference.

To keep the sun off your head, or maintain warmth in cooler temperatures, a simple cap or woolly hat/beanie works well. A watersports helmet is also a useful bit of kit for when you are near rocks or in fast-moving water.

For hands there are really three options. Neoprene gloves work in the same way as a wetsuit, but can leave you feeling

TOP Gloves, pogies and palmless mitts.

ABOVE A selection of water shoes.

disconnected from the paddle. For kayaks, there are Pogies – 'pockets' that fit around the shaft of the paddle that you put your hands into, leaving them warm and dry.

Finally, a good all-round option is neoprene palm-less mitts. Worn like a glove, the palm is open so you can still feel the paddle, while your fingers are protected from the cold as they wrap around it. You can also slide your fingers and thumbs out if you need to without removing the gloves.

There are many options for footwear, from bespoke kayaking boots and SUP shoes to simple beach shoes. Neoprene boots, shoes and socks can all be used separately or in layers, as can thermal and dry socks. If you choose to go barefoot while paddling, it may be worth taking footwear with you for when you're on land, especially on a beach or rocky area.

What to take

Everyone will have their own preference when it comes to kit to take on a paddle, and it will also be season dependent. But here is a brief kit list to help you pack the essentials.

- Means of contact: mobile phone in a waterproof case, very high frequency (VHF) radio (if you have a licence)
- Licence for the stretch of water you are paddling on (see guide to licences, page 12)
- Buoyancy aid or floatation device
- Suitable clothing for the weather (see guide to what to wear, page 6)
- Dry bag with spare dry clothes
- First aid kit
- Tag on your craft with name and number
- Food and drink

Prior to your paddle:
- Check the weather and the wind.
- Check the tides if paddling on tidal water.
- Check all your kit to make sure it is all fit for purpose and there is no damage.

Finally, make sure you clean down your kit after every paddle to prevent cross-contamination of rivers.

Guide to safety

Difficulty rating Throughout this book we have marked the paddles with a simple-to-follow rating for difficulty. These ratings are based on paddling in good weather, with low wind and normal conditions (i.e. river not in flood) and are a guide to complexity for a paddler with a little experience.

For people new to paddling we advise taking a lesson before you hit the water, and to always paddle with someone with more experience and/or local knowledge.

The ratings are:
- 💧 **Easy:** small lake, low-flowing river and short distances, beachside paddling
- 💧💧 **Moderate:** faster-flowing river, tidal medium distance, tidal estuary
- 💧💧💧 **Difficult:** open sea, fast-flowing water/tide crossing navigational lanes, complex route

Personal floatation devices (PFD)

Paddle UK (formerly British Canoeing), the national governing body for all forms of paddling, issued the following guidance in 2023 for stand up paddleboarding:

'Paddle UK strongly recommends that you have a primary form of floatation, which is normally your board via a leash AND a secondary form of floatation in the form of a buoyancy aid (BA) or personal floatation device (PFD). No matter which type of PFD you use, make sure it has the ISO 12402-5 or ISO 12402-6 certification. This means it passes all the necessary tests to be an effective and safe PFD.'

Full details can be found at: https://gopaddling.info/should-i-wear-a-buoyancy-aid-when-stand-up-paddle-boarding/

Kayakers and canoeists usually wear some form of PFD as they are not usually attached to the craft with a leash, and it can fill with

ABOVE A selection of personal floatation devices.

water. Surfers tend not to wear a PFD so that they can duck a wave etc., which could equally apply to SUP surfing.

How to choose a PFD The type of PFD you choose really depends on the application and the risk you are trying to mitigate. For example, some will not keep you face up in the water if you are unconscious and some require user interaction to inflate and deploy. Choose the one suitable for the craft you are paddling. A sit-in kayaker usually has a much shorter and more padded PFD, while a paddleboarder should avoid buckles and pockets on the front as these may hinder self-rescue. This may mean owning a few different styles.

Some inflatable waist-style PFDs need to be unpacked, put over your head and then inflated, and will need to be refitted with a gas canister each time they are operated, so be sure to carry some spares with you.

The best advice is to research the different types and try them for fitment and operation BEFORE you need to rely on them or use them in an emergency.

Leashes Paddle UK states the following regarding the use of leashes for paddlesports:

'The growth of stand up paddleboarding over recent years has been nothing short of phenomenal. But such sporadic growth also leaves room for safety mishaps. Stand up paddle boards have seen their fair share of controversy. BA or no BA? Ankle leash? Calf leash or Waist leash? Quick release or regular Velcro? With so many questions and misinformation circulating around the use of leashes and TYPES of leashes when stand up paddleboarding, we thought we would try and make it simple.'

Full details of Paddle UK's advice can be found here: https://gopaddling.info/stand-up-paddle-board-leashes/

The only point we at East of England Paddlesports would add is that combining a quick-release waist leash with a belt-type PFD adds the risk of one hindering the operation of the other. There are options to use a quick-release leash without a belt and combine it with a belt PFD to increase safety, one example of which can be found here: www.nrseurope.com/product/50008.03/nrs-quick-release-sup-leash.

Licences

This subject is often a point of contention for people in the paddling community. The arguments range from 'you don't need a licence to walk/ride a bike, so why would you need one to paddle public water' to 'we understand where the money goes and it's good value'.

Here at East of England Paddlesports we think acquiring the proper licence is all part of being a safe, responsible paddler. They are policed, and over the years we've been checked by river wardens, park rangers and the Environment Agency on numerous occasions, and there are reports of paddlers being fined up to £600 for unlicensed use.

If that wasn't enough to put you off paddling unlicensed, there is the incentive that, in all cases, the money goes back into gaining access to the water (remember, a lot of our rivers go through private land), maintaining the water and improving facilities at the water's edge, for example portage points.

We are frequently asked whether or not a licence is needed, or which licence to purchase, so we produced this short guide to help people through what can be a complicated area.

NOTE: each of the links and prices below were correct at the time of writing, and you can use them to check which licence covers where you are paddling. We have selected information that focuses on the East of England area.

Most tidal water is free to paddle on but there are exceptions to this. For example, the entire **Crouch Estuary** (including Foulness and the creeks) is within the jurisdiction of the Crouch Harbour Authority, which requires that all unpowered craft (canoes, kayaks, SUPs, inflatables, windsurfers, kitesurfers) are registered with them annually. Fees are £5.48 for a single craft, £10.96 for two to four, and £27.40 for five or more.
https://crouchharbour.uk/harbour-dues-canoe-kayak-paddle.../

Paddle UK is the most widely used and probably covers the most water. Membership includes a Waterways Licence and public liability insurance, and all income generated by membership fees is reinvested back into paddlesports, supporting the development of resources and projects that benefit members and the paddling community. The fee is between £47 and £60 per year for an adult (£85 for a couple, and family deals between £68 and £129). Membership covers the person and any craft they paddle. There are also offers, discounts and other benefits.
https://paddleuk.org.uk/waterways-licences/

If you only want to paddle on the **River Stour**, you can purchase a licence from the River Stour Trust. It's £5.50 per day, £11.50 for a week, £21.80 for a month or £48.60 for the year. This is for the craft, not the person. Remember, this is for one river, which the Paddle UK Waterways Licence covers. www.riverstourtrust.org/.../craft-registrations/

INTRODUCTION

Some rivers, like the Chelmer, require separate licensing. These are £6 per day or £41 per year, and can be purchased at the link below. Licence fees apply to all non-powered craft including dinghies and inflatables and it is not covered within other types of membership or licence. This licence applies to the craft, not the person. If you paddle a canoe, kayak or stand up paddleboard you will need to purchase a separate licence.
https://essexwaterways.com/licences

The non-tidal section of the River Colne through Colchester is one of those unusual rivers (like the Chelmer) that is private and not covered by the Paddle UK Licence. Colchester Borough Council own riparian rights to the river and its banks through this section are patrolled by rangers and do not offer a public licence or general access. Colchester Canoe Club has for many years been working with the council to improve facilities and access for all forms of watersports and as such their members and guests have been granted exclusive rights to use the river. Adult club membership is £30 per year and includes a locked private car park and, of course, river access. https://colchestercanoeclub.co.uk/

The Canal & River Trust license gives access to 96 canals and navigable rivers. Its website is difficult to use, in our opinion – it takes you to a very complicated registration and log in, where prices and how to license are both unclear. The licence page points you towards Paddle UK anyway, and the good news is a Paddle UK Licence covers membership for all CRT waterways.
https://canalrivertrust.org.uk/.../licensing-your-canoe.

The Broads National Park (or the Norfolk Broads, as many people call it) is controlled by the Broads Authority. The licence to paddle is available for £10.45 for a week, £20.90 for two weeks, or £46.32 for the year. This is for the craft, not per person. Again, if you already have Paddle UK membership you are covered to paddle here. www.broads-authority.gov.uk/.../owning-a-boat/tolls.

Another separate requirement is parts of waters covered by Anglian Waterways, which is generally more towards Cambridgeshire and includes the Ancholme, Black Sluice, Glen, Welland, Nene, Great Ouse System and Stour and covers backwaters, marinas and private moorings. While the Stour and parts of the Nene and Ouse are covered by other licences mentioned above, parts of the Great Ouse and Nene are not. You can check the requirements on the Paddle UK website. If needed for other sections, then this licence is per craft and covers kayaks, canoes and stand up paddleboards. The price is £5.40 per day, £11.30 per week, £18.70 for a 15 Day Explorer, £21.40 per month, or £47.70 per year.
www.gov.uk/government/publications/anglian-waterways-registration-charges/anglian-waterways-boat-registration-and-other-charges-1-april-2022-to-31-march-2023#unpowered-open-boats

Some areas like the River Cam through Cambridge city centre require your licence number to be displayed and visible from the riverbank, so please be sure to investigate all oddities before taking to the water.
www.camconservancy.org/canoeing

We also have many lakes in the East of England area. Most are privately owned or owned by water companies. Each has its own pricing for launch or hiring and most require third-party insurance, which as you can see above comes with many of the licences already covered here.

ESSEX

Where coastlines collide with history. Unfurl a map of England's southeast, and your gaze will fall upon Essex, a county where the North Sea whispers secrets to rolling farmlands. This vibrant region boasts a rich tapestry woven from its dramatic coastline, charming towns and a history that stretches back centuries.

Essex's defining feature is undoubtedly its staggering 562 miles of coastline, the longest of any English county. For a dose of classic English seaside charm, head to Southend-on-Sea, with its bustling pier and traditional amusements. Nature lovers will find solace on the peaceful marshlands of the Essex Coast, designated National Landscapes, where diverse birdlife thrives. History buffs will be enthralled by Essex's rich heritage. Colchester, Britain's first Roman capital, boasts a magnificent Roman wall and the ruins of its famed temple. Explore the grand Norman-era Colchester Castle, a testament to the county's strategic significance. Beyond Roman and medieval influences, wander the ancient woodlands of Epping Forest, a sprawling expanse that has served as a hunting ground for royalty for centuries.

While the North Sea takes centre stage, Essex isn't without its rivers. The majestic River Thames forms the county's southern border, offering stunning riverside walks and boat trips. Several tributaries snake through the Essex countryside, including the River Crouch, a haven for sailing and watersports enthusiasts. Explore the charming harbour towns that dot the riversides, each with its own unique character and maritime history.

Beyond the historical gems and natural beauty, Essex offers a delightful mix of urban and rural life. Explore the vibrant city of Chelmsford, the county town, with its buzzing high street and cultural offerings. Venture into the charming market towns like Saffron Walden, famed for its saffron history and timber-framed buildings. For a quintessential English village experience, explore the picture-perfect villages scattered throughout the county, each with its own pub, church and sense of community.

Essex is a county that caters to every whim. Whether you seek adventure on the dramatic coastline, historical intrigue in its ancient towns, or a tranquil escape amidst rolling hills and rivers, Essex promises an unforgettable experience.

ABOVE Ted on the beach.

RIGHT Sunrise at Dovercourt Lighthouse.

01 BRIGHTLINGSEA TO WIVENHOE

Brightlingsea is located on the Colne Estuary 16km from Colchester town. This little seaside town is a perfect location to go for a paddle, but as it is tidal waters, the wind and the tide must be considered beforehand. As well as paddling around Brightlingsea, and the creeks that surround it (see page 30), it is possible to paddle upriver to Wivenhoe, Rowhedge or to the Mersea Strood via Pyefleet Creek.

The Lowdown

DISTANCE Up to 16km

WATER TYPE Tidal estuary

DIFFICULTY 💧💧 to 💧💧💧 depending on conditions

LICENCE REQUIRED ✗

PARKING All car parks located in Brightlingsea, except Wivenhoe public pontoon:
Tower Street CO7 0AP, ///beanbag.repaying.clauses. Free for 2 hr. 28 spaces. Also roadside parking near Town Hard, however can flood with high tide.
Oyster Tank Road CO7 0DW, ///caressing.frost.players. 150 spaces.
West Prom Grass Western Promenade CO7 0HH, ///loafing.captive.glory. 300 spaces. Height barrier 1.98m.
Promenade Way CO7 0HH, ///condense.fame.songs. 64 spaces.
Wivenhoe public pontoon CO7 9GS, ///starts.lengthen.petulant. Limited parking for a small charge.
All car parks pay and display at time of writing.

LAUNCH POINTS Town hard jetty ///possible.grumbling.expand. Accessible at both high and low tide.
Wivenhoe public pontoon ///nibbled.salmon.frog.

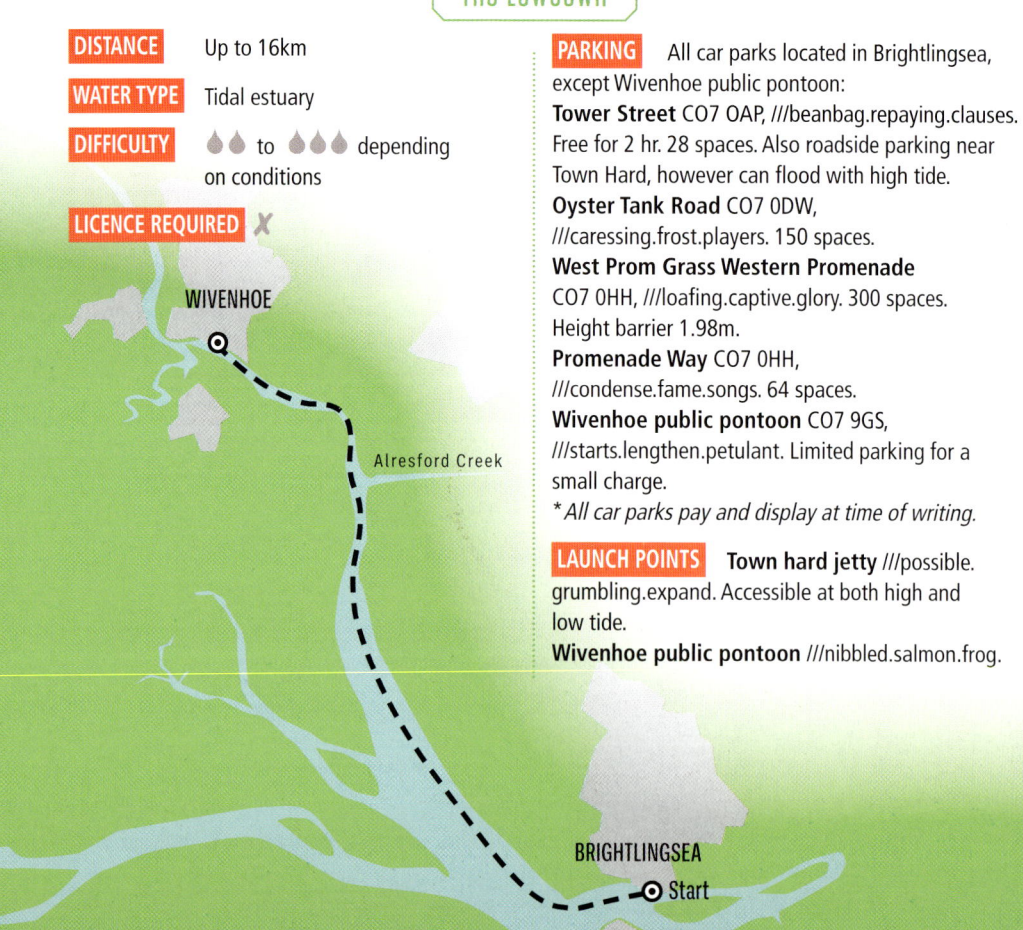

BRIGHTLINGSEA TO WIVENHOE

History

Brightlingsea was an island in the 16th century. It is perhaps best known for its connection with the Confederation of the Cinque Ports. The Cinque Ports were five ports on the south-east coast of England (Hastings, Sandwich, Dover, Romney and Hythe), established by Royal Charter in 1155 to maintain ships and men for war in case of need. As a thriving ship port, Brightlingsea was chosen as a Limb Port of the Head Port of Sandwich.

Wivenhoe was developed as a port in the 18th century. It has a rich history of boatbuilding, including smacks and cargo vessels. Wivenhoe, like Brightlingsea, is also famed for its oyster and fishing industries. This being said, it is quite important to wear shoes when walking or paddling on this stretch of coast, as the oyster shells are very sharp and found everywhere on the beach and in the mud.

The paddle

This paddle is not suitable for beginners, as the tide, wind, swell and distance must all be considered. Allow at least 3–4 hours before high tide to launch from Brightlingsea, so that the incoming tide will assist you with your paddle to Wivenhoe. You can do this paddle either one way to Wivenhoe, or if you wish to paddle back to Brightlingsea, ensure you allow time to return, ideally as the tide turns to let the outgoing tide assist you back to your starting point.

Tide height must also be considered, as it becomes very shallow and muddy on this stretch just before you enter Wivenhoe. Therefore, ensure you undertake this paddle when there is a good amount of water (check tide heights before you leave).

To paddle this route, launch at Brightlingsea from the town jetty and keep to the right. You will then paddle past Splash Point and Bateman's Tower on your right (to the left is Mersea Island, where you will see the mouth of Pyefleet Creek).

You will then be heading down the Colne Estuary towards Wivenhoe. As you follow this river you'll pass Fingringhoe Wick Nature Discovery Park to the left, and you'll

RIGHT Structure at entrance of Alresford Creek where it meets the River Colne.

BELOW Aerial shot of Wivenhoe and Rowhedge.

see the entrance of Alresford Creek to the right, with a metal structure.

The river then bends to the left and this leads you to the Colne Tide Barrier. Once you paddle past it, to the right is the public pontoon, in which you can land and portage.

If you wish to carry on a little further, you'll go past Wivenhoe front to Rowhedge village, then to the Hythe, which ends the tidal section of the Colne Estuary.

Alresford Creek You'll pass Alresford Creek to your right just before you get into Wivenhoe. This creek is a beautiful paddle; it's best to time it with the incoming tide to help you, while this also ensures that there is enough water – as with all the other creek paddles on this estuary, it can become shallow and muddy.

Bearing in mind the mud, this paddle is best to do when high tide height is high. If it's due to be a low/neep tide, then best to avoid, as you'll launch in the thick mud and won't be able to paddle far down the creek. The launch point for this specific paddle is ///likewise.magazine.shuttered and there is parking space on Ford Lane (///paddle.panicking.glory) for around four cars with no height barriers. At the time of writing parking is free; however, beware of the tide, which can come up the road on a very high tide/spring tide.

Wildlife As there is both a nature reserve and marshland on this paddle, you should see plenty of wildlife! Saltmarshes provide a rich feeding ground for migratory waders in spring and autumn, while in the winter you'll hear the distinctive '*ruk-ruk-ruk*' of brent geese. Terns can often be seen on the shingle sandbank alongside some other coastal birds, such as oystercatchers, wagtails, swans and many others.

Fingringhoe Wick Nature Discovery Park is managed by Essex Wildlife Trust. It is known for its nightingales in the spring, with 1 per cent of the UK population breeding on the reserve before heading back to Africa for the winter. Birdsong from chiffchaffs, whitethroat and cuckoos can also be heard from the reserve. In the

RIGHT Alresford Creek at low tide.
BELOW Splashpoint in Brightlingsea.

summer, you might see marsh harriers, turtle doves, sand martins and swallows, while in autumn there are avocets and turnstones.

From the water, you may even see the odd seal or two popping their heads up – or even a porpoise!

Food stops There are plenty of food stops in both Brightlingsea and Wivenhoe, with both towns offering supermarkets, cafés, restaurants, pubs, fish and chip shops, and bakeries.

Other activities Wivenhoe offers a ferry to Rowhedge and Fingringhoe, which runs most weekends during April to October. It is run entirely by volunteers.

If you fancy a walk, run or bike ride, the Wivenhoe Trail starts by Wivenhoe train station and goes all the way to Castle Park in Colchester. Along this route there is also a beautiful woodland area to explore.

The Nottage Maritime Institute is located next to the river. For more information visit: www.nottage.org.uk.

RIGHT Reed beds along Arlesford creek.

BELOW Thorrington Tide Mill at the end of Arlesford Creek.

NEED TO KNOW

■ As this is a tidal section of the Colne Estuary, you don't need a licence to paddle, but timing is critical for launch (see page 12 for more information).

■ Toilet facilities available down Promenade Way.

■ No dogs on the beach May–September, and they must be kept on lead.

■ Ensure you check the tide times before paddling, as most locations, except the Town Hard, can only be launched at high tide.

■ Check the wind speed and direction before setting off. Please ensure to paddle within your capabilities.

■ Footwear is essential due to the oyster shells along the coastline in Brightlingsea.

02 CHELMER AND BLACKWATER NAVIGATION

This is a popular spot with paddlers of all crafts. There are multiple places to launch along the River Chelmer. The stretch we've chosen to highlight here runs from Chelmsford City to Heybridge, and you can choose to paddle the complete stretch, which equates to 22.1km, or from lock to lock. There are 13 locks from the Springfield Basin to the sea, and a lot of wildlife to be seen along the way, including a variety of birds and even terrapins!

The Lowdown

DISTANCE 1–17km

WATER TYPE River

DIFFICULTY 💧 to 💧💧 depending on the distance chosen to paddle

LICENCE REQUIRED  (see Need to know box)

PARKING Chelmsford: multiple parking sites in town, but the two nearest to the Springfield Basin launch point are:
Horizon Parking 2 Hanbury Rd, CM2 6LUX, ///lungs.detail.fires. No height restrictions.
Meadows Retail Wharf Rd CM2 6LU, ///active.baked.order). No barriers or height restrictions.
Daisy Meadow Basin Road, Heybridge CM9 4RW, ///patrolled.niece.shampoo. No height restrictions. Approx. 130 spaces.
All car parks pay and display at time of writing.

LAUNCH POINTS
Springfield Basin ///bland.kept.hook
Papermill Lock in the direction of Heybridge launch at ///passions.engineers.cases; in the direction of Chelmsford launch at ///debate.bogus.chat
Daisy Meadow Heybridge, ///ordinary.notebook.structure

CHELMSFORD Start
DANBURY
HEYBRIDGE

East of England Paddlesports hosted an event on this stretch, during which more than 20 of our members paddled the entire length of the navigation from Chelmsford to Heybridge, stopping at Papermill Lock tea rooms en route for a spot of lunch. It was a fab day out!

ABOVE Sunrise on the Chelmer.

BELOW RIGHT Matt paddling under the Chelmer Road bridge at an EOEPs event.

BELOW Paddling out of Chelmsford town.

History

The Chelmer and Blackwater Navigation runs for 22km from Springfield Basin in Chelmsford to the sea lock at Heybridge Basin near Maldon. Before the Eastern Counties Railway from London to Colchester was constructed in 1843, the waterway carried a range of materials and goods. However, once the railway was built the use of the waterway declined, but coal continued to be imported until the First World War. The sea lock at Heybridge was enlarged after the Second World War, but

trade gradually declined and ceased in 1972.

In 1973, the Inland Waterways Association held a Rally of Boats in Chelmsford and this set the scene for opening the waterways up for pleasure craft.

The paddle

The Chelmer and Blackwater Navigation starts in Chelmsford and ends in Heybridge. The complete paddle is 22km, but there are multiple launch points and paddle spots to make this accessible for all skill abilities. To do this navigation one way, you'll need to organise a shuttle, ideally with a vehicle at the end point in Heybridge and another to take you to Chelmsford to start the paddle (park at one of the car parks mentioned in the panel on page 21).

The locks starting from Chelmsford are: Springfield Lock and Basin, Barnes Mill, Sandford, Cuton, Stonham's, Little Baddow Mill, Papermill, Rushes, Hoe Mill, Ricketts, Beeleigh, Langford Cut, Heybridge Basin and Sea. You cannot pass through these locks on paddlecraft, so all craft must portage at each lock. Visit www.waterways.org.uk for more information on each lock and launch point.

From Chelmsford, you can launch from Springfield Basin (///bland.kept.hook).

As you paddle out of Chelmsford, you will approach Springfield Lock, which you'll need to portage around. Continuing on out of Chelmsford you'll go under the Chelmer Road bridge. Once you leave the hustle and bustle of Chelmsford you'll suddenly notice you're surrounded by farmland and nature.

There are multiple locks and portage points on this route, but go past Barnes Mill, Sandford, Cuton, Stonham's and Little Baddow Mill locks, and you'll finally reach Papermill Lock.

Papermill Lock is a popular area for people to stop, as a tea room here offers delicious food and drinks. There's also a car park here, open May–September. This can be a busy area as there are boat rides, canal boats and hikers, so please be mindful of other water users at all times. There's also a weir, which is beautiful to see and paddle past. You can also park and launch at this location; the tea room opens its car park (North Hill, Little Baddow CM3 4BS, ///dilute.masks.scores) to customers and there is a charge for parking. There is very limited on-road parking.

BELOW Matt, Oli and Jess at Papermill Lock.

RIGHT All Saints Church, Ulting.

BELOW Matt paddling under Elms Farm Park Bridge in Maldon.

FAR RIGHT Paddles Up! On the Chelmer Navigation paddle event with EOEPS.

You will need to portage Papermill Lock. The portage point is located by the slipway. Once out, walk past the tea rooms and as you pass the weir there's a portage point before the road, and you will then see the weir across the river, which makes for a beautiful backdrop.

Once past Papermill Lock, continue along the Chelmer. You may spot some beautiful sights along this route, including All Saints Church in Ulting, on the left before you approach Hoe Mill Lock.

If you're continuing to Heybridge Basin, continue paddling along the Chelmer. Eventually you will be met with a fork in the route. Stick to the left, which you'll then be portaging at Beeleigh Lock. This is a lovely area to pause and have a sit, although there's a road here so please be mindful of moving traffic. Once you've portaged you'll notice the rural, nature-filled paddle changes again, to a paddle through Maldon Town. This section is quite straightforward and takes you past houses and a Tesco supermarket, before you reach Heybridge Basin, where there are lots of boats. Daisy Meadows car park is to the left, situated behind the small Daisy Meadows Kiosk, and this is also where the portage point is.

Wildlife

This route takes you through the rural Essex countryside, so there is an abundance of wildlife to be spotted, including lapwings, which tend to surround the farmers' fields during breeding season, kingfishers, herons, bats and game birds.

The dominant tree species for most of the Chelmer and Blackwater Navigation is a specialist variety of willow, the cricket bat willow.

Food stops

There are multiple cafés, restaurants and pubs in Chelmsford town centre, a short walk from Springfield Basin, while the tea rooms at Papermill Lock and Heybridge Basin provide refreshments for weary paddlers.

Other activities

You'll be spoilt for choice in Chelmsford, one of the UK's newest cities, having been granted city

CHELMER AND BLACKWATER NAVIGATION

status in 2012. You'll find a cinema, ice skating rink, swimming pools, bowling and plentiful shopping to keep you busy after a long paddle.

There is also the option to hire craft from the tea rooms at Papermill Lock, or embark on a short boat ride on the canal.

Heybridge Basin is not far from Maldon town, which has a busy promenade and high street.

For open water swimming and cycling, try Trifarm in Boreham (https://trifarm.co.uk/).

NEED TO KNOW

- Paddlers must pay for a licence before launching. Day or annual licences can be purchased online at www.waterways.org.uk, or in Heybridge at the Daisy Meadow Kiosk (CM9 4RY, ///parkland.slime.yappy) during opening hours (see page 12 for more information).

- This stretch of river is used by pleasure craft, so take care and observe the keep right rule for paddling.

- Paddlers must not pass through the locks – there are landing stages above and below each lock which you can portage on. This stretch is also used by motorboats, and paddlers must follow the river code and pass on the right.

- Paddlers must take care around and avoid weirs.

03 DOVERCOURT BAY

Dovercourt is situated on the North Essex coast near Harwich. It is known for its twin lighthouses, which make for a beautiful backdrop for any paddling photo, especially during sunrise.

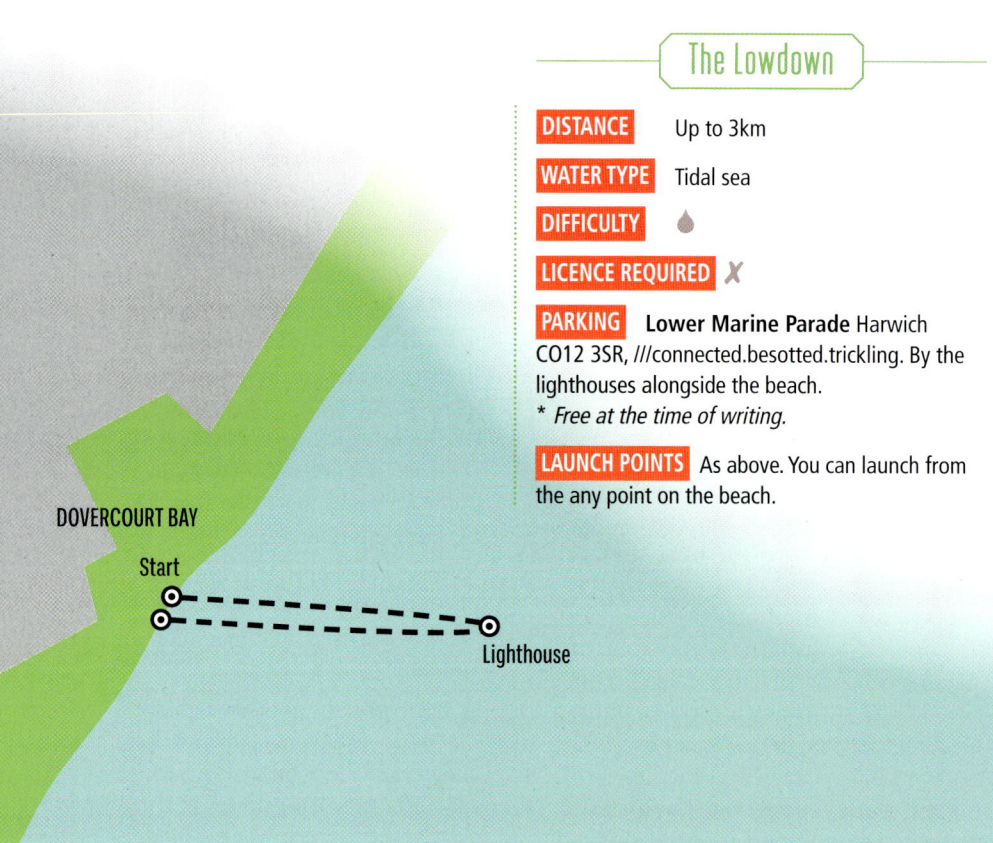

The Lowdown

DISTANCE Up to 3km

WATER TYPE Tidal sea

DIFFICULTY 💧

LICENCE REQUIRED ✗

PARKING **Lower Marine Parade** Harwich CO12 3SR, ///connected.besotted.trickling. By the lighthouses alongside the beach.
* Free at the time of writing.

LAUNCH POINTS As above. You can launch from the any point on the beach.

RIGHT Jess getting some blue therapy watching the sunrise at Dovercourt.

As this is a tidal location, planning is key. The beach is only accessible at high tide and, with it being the open sea, it is essential you check the wind and weather before setting off. But with perfect conditions this paddle is hard to beat. By no means is it a long trip, but it's a relaxing, pretty place to get some blue therapy.

East of England Paddlesports regularly host sunrise and paddle events here. We have the most magnificent turnouts for sunrise paddles, and it's the best way to start the day!

History

Dovercourt is known for its twin lighthouses – cast iron towers that were built in 1863 and in operation until 1917, guiding vessels around Languard Point. The differing heights of the lighthouses (15m and 4m) allowed the lights to be aligned as vessels approached, indicating the correct course. With the introduction of marker buoys, the lighthouses became obsolete and fell into disrepair, although they were restored in the 1980s.

The paddle

Park at Lower Marine Parade and launch from anywhere on the beach. The paddle to the lighthouse itself is by no means a long one; however, it can be magical, especially if you're lucky to catch a sunrise in perfect conditions, where the pinky-orange colours in the sky reflect in the sea. The lighthouses create such a wonderful backdrop, making this paddle hard to beat.

You can paddle along the coastline, however, there's a busy shipping channel down towards Harwich, so care must be taken in this area. It is not recommended to paddle past 'The Point', where you will see the breakwater, as this signifies entry to the busy shipping channel.

Wildlife

Both common and grey seals can be spotted in the area, and with Hamford Water, a biological Site of Special Scientific Interest, just around the corner, you may notice the seals have a slight orange tinge. This is due to the iron oxide they pick up from the muddy marshes in the nearby estuary.

Wagtails can also be spotted on the beach, hopping from one spot to another, 'wagging' their tail feathers.

Although paddlers often visit this location at high tide, at low tide you can go rock pooling, and you may find an array of shells and sea life, such as sea anemones and starfish.

Food stops
As Dovercourt is a town, there is an abundance of shops, cafés and fish and chip shops nearby, including a large supermarket and a fast food chain.

Other activities
Harwich is the next town along from Dovercourt. Here you can visit the Ha'penny Pier (View Point Road, ///observers.bottled.gambles), the RNLI station and Harwich Redoubt Fort. There is also a foot ferry which connects Harwich to Shotley and Felixstowe, in Suffolk. The ferry operates every day in favourable weather between 1 April and 31 October.

> ### NEED TO KNOW
>
> ■ As this is the North Sea and not a river, you don't require a licence to paddle, but timing is critical for launch (see page 12 for more information).
>
> ■ Care must be taken when paddling on tidal water. Please check local tide times as well as the daily wind forecast before setting off. Please paddle within your own capabilities.
>
> ■ Harwich has a busy shipping channel and it is not recommended to paddle past 'The Point', where you will see the breakwater as this enters the busy shipping channel.

RIGHT The glowing sky and lighthouse.

04 BRIGHTLINGSEA ESTUARY AND THE CREEKS

Brightlingsea is located on the Colne Estuary, 16km from Colchester town. This little seaside town is a perfect location to go for a paddle, but as it is tidal waters, the wind and the tide must be considered beforehand. There are various paddling options available depending on your wants and ability, including paddles close to shore, and exploring the various creeks and marshes that surround the area.

The Lowdown

DISTANCE Varies

WATER TYPE Tidal estuary

DIFFICULTY Varied depending on conditions and route

LICENCE REQUIRED ✗

PARKING All car parks located in Brightlingsea:
Tower Street CO7 0AP, ///beanbag.repaying.clauses. Free for 2 hr. 28 spaces. Also roadside parking near Town Hard, however can flood with high tide.
Oyster Tank Road CO7 0DW, ///caressing.frost.players. 150 spaces.
West Prom Grass Western Promenade CO7 0HH, ///loafing.captive.glory. 300 spaces. Height barrier 1.98m.
Promenade Way CO7 0HH, ///condense.fame.songs. 64 spaces.
All car parks pay and display at time of writing.

LAUNCH POINTS **Town hard jetty**, ///possible.grumbling.expand. Accessible at both high and low tide.
Bateman's Tower ///grab.elbow.commander. Accessible at high tide.
Splashpoint ///tall.duet.appoints. Accessible at high tide.
Promenade* ///populate.peroxide.woke. Accessible at high tide.
* NOTE the ramp is privately owned by the sailing club.

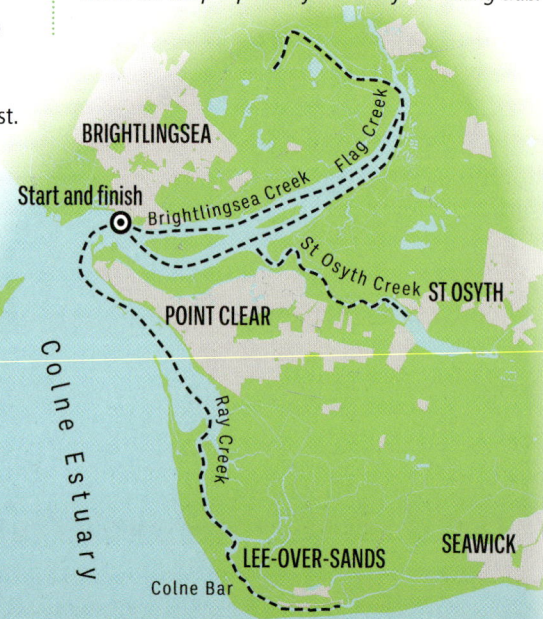

BRIGHTLINGSEA ESTUARY AND THE CREEKS

History

Brightlingsea was an island in the 16th century. It is perhaps best known for its connection with the Confederation of the Cinque Ports. The Cinque Ports were five ports on the south-east coast of England (Hastings, Sandwich, Dover, Romney and Hythe), established by Royal Charter in 1155 to maintain ships and men for war in case of need. As a thriving ship port, Brightlingsea was chosen as a Limb Port of the Head Port of Sandwich.

It is now a busy fishing port, with oyster beds along the creek (which can be seen on a low tide), and often you can see the oyster trawlers out on the creek, harvesting their catch. This being said, it is quite important to wear shoes when walking or paddling on this stretch of coast, as the oyster shells are very sharp and found everywhere on the beach and in the mud.

The paddle

Brightlingsea is situated just at the mouth of the Colne Estuary. There are endless options for paddles from Brightlingsea, from the creeks covered below, to heading to the Mersea Strood by paddling down Pyefleet Creek, or undertaking a longer paddle to Wivenhoe following the Colne Estuary. Point Clear and East Mersea are situated opposite Brightlingsea when looking out from the promenade. This is what makes Brightlingsea such a great place to paddle, as it caters for all abilities and skills, as long as the conditions and tide are on your side! It is also a particularly beautiful area to paddle in at both sunrise and sunset.

It is advisable to paddle on a high tide around the creeks, but it is possible to launch from the town jetty at a low tide and head out of the estuary, where there will still be enough water to paddle around.

The creeks and surrounding towns

Brightlingsea is surrounded by multiple creeks, including Brightlingsea, St Osyth, Ray

BELOW Aerial Shot of Brightlingsea Harbour.

LEFT Sunset in Brightlingsea.
ABOVE The shell on Point Clear Bay.
RIGHT Boats in Brightlingsea Creek.

and Flag. Most creeks can only be accessed fully at high tide. Due to the muddy nature of the Colne Estuary, the creeks become shallow and muddy, too; therefore, planning your paddle around high tide is advisable. All creeks can be accessed via any of the launch points listed above.

Brightlingsea Creek can only be paddled to the end on a high tide. To access the creek, launch from any of the launch points and head left. You will then see the marina and town jetty to your left, with boat moorings and Point Clear on your right. This is the entrance of Brightlingsea Creek.

As you enter, you will see that the creek has two routes. It is advisable to paddle the left route, as the right side has lots of boat moorings. As you paddle down the left route, you will pass the port and may come across an enormous container ship and Morgan Marine boat yard.

As you paddle past Morgan Marine, you will notice an island to your right. This island actually consists of two islands called 'Cindery 1 and Cindery 2', which provide a nesting and resting area for seabirds.

As you head down to the end of the creek, it leads to a narrow creek called **Flag Creek**, which is very shallow and can only be accessed at high waters. (Please ensure to check the tide height as this can become too shallow to pass if on a neep tide.)

To explore **St Osyth Creek**, head left from any of the launch points towards Brightlingsea Creek. The route splits in two by Cindery Islands. Take the route on the right, where you'll see a number of boat moorings. Please be mindful paddling around this area, as it can be busy with boat traffic.

As you pass Cindery Island 1 you'll see a creek entrance to the right. This is St Osyth Creek. The creek leads to St Osyth village and ends at St Osyth Boatyard. The boatyard is privately owned, so you cannot land.

Point Clear Bay and Ray Creek are situated to the south of Brightlingsea. Head out of the harbour towards the estuary. Bearing to the left you will find Point Clear, and behind the shingle you'll find Point Clear Bay and Lagoon.

Enter the lagoon and Ray Creek is the first creek to the right. It is advisable to paddle this creek on an incoming tide, to ensure you have enough time to paddle to the end

and the small coastal hamlet of Lee-over-Sands. You should then be able to return on the outward tide. The current can be very strong on this stretch, so plan ahead and monitor tide and wind conditions. This creek is surrounded by a Colne Point Nature Reserve, which is the perfect place for some birdwatching.

Wildlife

The coastline that hugs Brightlingsea and the surrounding area is a mixture of shingle beaches, exposed mudflats, shell banks and salt marshes, thus providing a rich feeding ground for migratory waders in spring and autumn, while in the winter you'll hear the distinctive 'ruk-ruk-ruk' of brent geese. Terns can often be seen on the shingle sandbank, alongside oystercatchers, wagtails, swans and many other coastal birds.

While paddling along the creeks you may also spot samphire growing. However, permission must be obtained if you are to harvest any, and if harvesting, it is important to cut the tops and not pull the roots out.

You may even spot some playful seals and porpoises while out paddling, making for an experience you'll never forget!

Food stops

There is an abundance of pubs, fish and chip shops, supermarkets, corner shops, restaurants and takeaway restaurants (Chinese, Thai and Indian) in Brightlingsea. There is also a food truck by Batemans Tower that serves chips, cakes, ice creams and drinks.

Other activities

Brightlingsea Museum is situated on Station Road (CO7 0DT, ///tumblers.whistle.draw). It reopened in new purpose-built premises in 2020 and is a fun day out for the whole family, with various trails and a souvenir shop. Open from Easter to December, free entry.

Brightlingsea Lido is a classic 1930s open-air swimming pool on Promenade Way (CO7 0HH, ///punters.marathon.laminate). There's a 50m (unheated) outdoor pool plus a smaller pool for toddlers. There's also a café on site. Booking is required, which you can do at their website: www.brightlinsealido.org. Open May to September.

Brightlingsea beach is a small beach area with a shallow humanmade pool that is filled twice a day by the tide and is suitable for children. This beach is right next to Batemans Tower and Splashpoint, both

ESSEX

great locations to do a spot of crabbing. Park at Promenade Way car park (CO7 0HH, ///condense.fame.songs).

Various events are held here during the summer, including Pyefleet Week regatta, Brightlingsea Food & Drink Festival, Brightlingsea Free Music Festival, and the Fresh Air Festival of Outdoor Arts. See https://visitbrightlingsea.co.uk/whats-on/ for more information.

Every September, traditional barges, smack boats and Mersea fishermans' open boats (MFOBs) line up for the Colne Smack & Barge Match, a race that starts and finishes at Batemans Tower – an amazing sight to see!

NEED TO KNOW

■ As this is a tidal section of the River Colne, you don't require a license to paddle, but timing is critical for launch (see page 12 for more information).

■ Toilet facilities available down Promenade Way.

■ No dogs on the beach May–September, and they must be kept on lead.

■ Ensure you check the tide times before paddling, as most locations, except the Town Hard, can only be launched at high tide.

■ Check the wind speed and direction before setting off. Please ensure to paddle within your capabilities.

■ Footwear is essential due to the oyster shells along the coastline in Brightlingsea.

TOP Batemans Tower.
LEFT Shipwreck in Brightlingsea Creek.
RIGHT Sunrise in Brightlingsea Creek.

05 SAWBRIDGEWORTH TO HARLOW

The Stort Valley meanders for 39km down to the River Lee at Feildes Weir in Hoddesdon, through a beautiful landscape of watermills and nature reserves. The railway line runs parallel with the river, so you can paddle the length of the River Stort and hop on the train back to your starting point.

The Lowdown

DISTANCE 6–13km

WATER TYPE River

DIFFICULTY ○

LICENCE REQUIRED ✓ (see Need to know box)

PARKING **Sheering Mill Lane** Sawbridgeworth, ///agrees.other.hungry. Free. Room for eight cars or vans. No height restrictions.

LAUNCH POINT **Sheering Mill** Lock, ///marble.oines.rotate. 1 min walk from parking (above). Walk towards the river and head right. Portage point is just by the cottage.

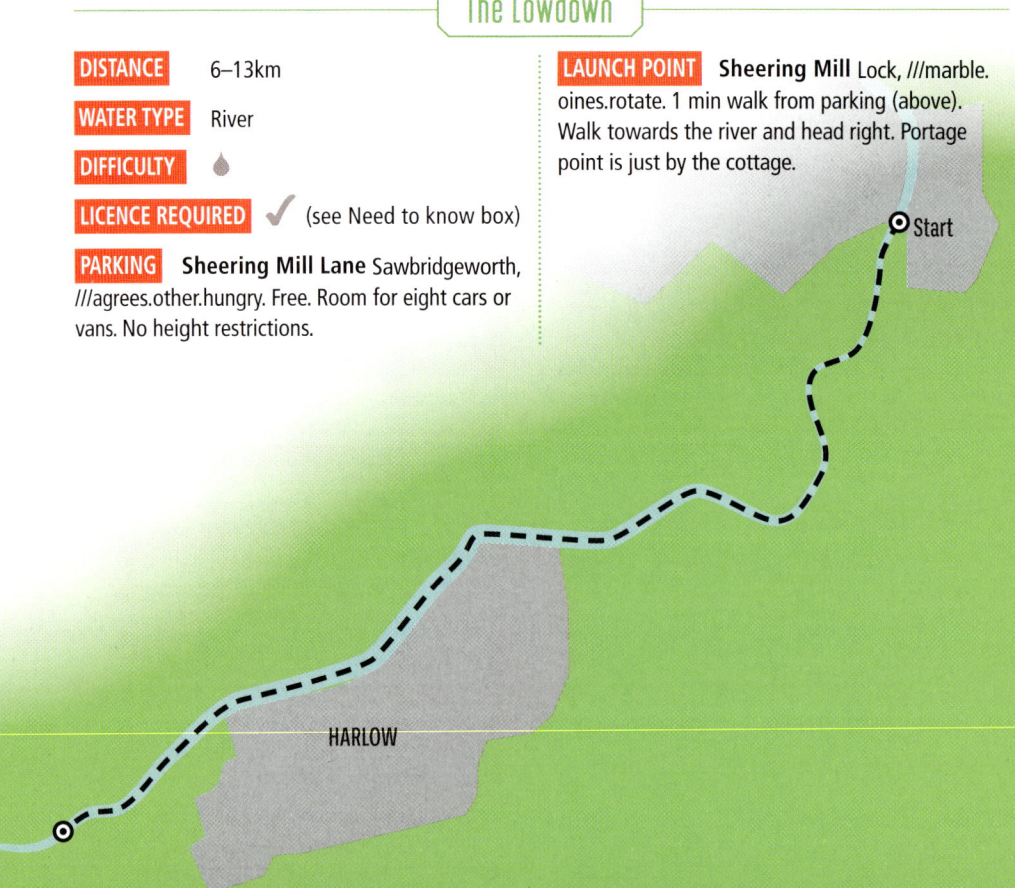

ABOVE Surrounded by nature on the River Stort.

History

Sawbridgeworth made its name through the local maltings (a building used to produce malt for brewing beer and whisky), which were situated on the river to enable the movement of malt via the River Stort. They were owned by George Fawbert and John Barnard who, in 1839, set up the Fawbert and Barnard charity to fund local children and their education, and a primary school that still exists today.

Much of the town centre is a conservation area, with many of its buildings dating back to the Tudor, Stuart and Georgian periods, while Great St Marys church was built in the 13th century.

Harlow is a much newer town, being the second new town to be built after the war, in 1947. But history can still be found here, with some buildings dating back to the Roman period – this is the site of a Roman temple dedicated to the goddess Minerva. It is also the birthplace of fibre optic telecommunications technology – it was invented in the early 1960s, at Telecommunication Laboratories in Harlow.

The paddle

This is a return paddle from Sawbridgeworth to Harlow, which equates to 13km. There are several portages along the way, which can drop in the drier seasons, so please take care when portaging. Portages are standard lock conditions, a mixture of grass verges and concrete hards with plenty of space to get in and out.

After entering the river, go right to head towards Harlow (there is also another portage point on the left which takes you in the direction of Bishop's Stortford). Between Sherring Mill Lock and Feakes Lock there are plenty of canal boats nestled in the banks – a beautiful sight. Not long after a footbridge you'll approach your first lock, Feakes, which you can portage either side.

Carrying on from Feakes Lock, the river meanders with a lot of bends and continues through woodland and nature reserves. It then becomes slightly more industrial when you reach the houses and apartments to the left.

You will then head under Cambridge Road and see the Harlow Mill Beefeater restaurant on the right-hand side (please note, there are no portage points or landing points at this location to get food or drink). Past this point, you'll arrive at Harlow Lock, which you will need to portage.

The next stretch between Harlow Lock and Latton Lock is more winding river and more industrious. You might be able to see Redricks Lake through the trees to your right depending on which season you choose to paddle this stretch. Once you arrive at Latton Lock, you'll need to portage it.

This is now the final stretch before Harlow, which is much like the previous stretch, with industrial sites to your left and fields and woodland to your right. As you approach Harlow Marsh, the river gets slightly wider. Further along this stretch you'll get the first sights of Moorhend Moorings, a private marina. As you pass this on the right, you'll then come to The Moorhen pub, the final destination for this paddle (although you can carry on up the River Stort!). The drop is bigger at this portage point, but once you get out there are public toilets and access to water outside the pub. The Moorhen is accessible to paddlers, with plenty of garden space for paddle craft, where you can sit and enjoy some much-earned refreshment!

Wildlife

Much like the Bishop's Stortford paddle (see page 180), there is plenty of wildlife to see on this trip, with nature reserves and farmland surrounding this stretch of the river.

The River Stort is also home to several RSPB Nature Reserves, including Bluebell Woods Rushy Meads, Bishop Stortford; Sawbridge Marsh, Sawbridgeworth; Pishiobury Park, Sawbridgeworth; and Gibbert Garden Harlow; and there is plenty of birdlife to be seen along the way, including mallards, moorhens, kingfishers, grey wagtails, herons, blackcaps, house martins, pied wagtails, starlings, coots, great spotted woodpeckers, goldfinch, mute swans, swallows, sparrowhawks and many more. With luck, you may also spot pipistrelle bats, water voles and even otters.

Food stops
The Moorhen pub in Harlow offers refreshments for weary paddlers and water access. Visit Moorhen Pub, Burntmill Lane, Harlow, CM20 2QS. ///beside.since.client (www.greenking.co.uk).

As this paddle starts and ends in towns, there are plenty of food stops at either end, including several pubs, coffee shops and supermarkets.

Other activities
There are plenty of activities to keep you busy in both Sawbridgeworth and Harlow. Tudor House Gallery is a gift shop that offers unique handmade jewellery, glassware, crafts, and ceramics (https://thetudorhouse.gallery), while Maltings Antiques has three floors of antiques and curios (www.maltingsantiques.co.uk/). If you're looking for something more lively, The Pinball Office is home to over 30 pinball machines and arcades, all set on free play (www.thepinballoffice.co.uk/).

Harlow Museum & Walled Gardens (www.harlowmuseum.com/) is packed with history and has three gardens to explore.

There are several options for canal boat day trips and local river cruises, or you can hire a canal boat.

ABOVE A frosty morning on the River Stort.
LEFT Feakes Lock.
BELOW The River Stort sign.

ESSEX

TOP Poppy the dog admiring the canal boats on the River Stort.

ABOVE Canal boats.

NEED TO KNOW

- Various Boat hires are available online. See Canal Ability (www.canalability.org.uk/canal-boat-day-trips) for more information.

- A licence is required to paddle the River Stort and can be obtained from Paddle UK (see page 12 for more information).

- This stretch of river is used by pleasure craft, so take care and observe the keep right rule for paddling.

06 DEDHAM TO FLATFORD

Arguably one of the most scenic places in Essex, Dedham is a beautiful village situated around 10km north-east of Colchester and 6.5km north-west of Manningtree. Dedham is a very popular spot due to its accessibility to the public and uninterrupted surroundings, being part of the Dedham Vale National Landscape.

The Lowdown

DISTANCE 5–12km

WATER TYPE River

DIFFICULTY 💧

LICENCE REQUIRED ✓ (see Need to know box)

PARKING **Mill Lane Car Park** ///himself.assess.displays, Mill lane Dedham, Colchester CO7.

LAUNCH POINT As above, ///adjusted.pylons.workloads. Concrete slipway with wooden pontoon.

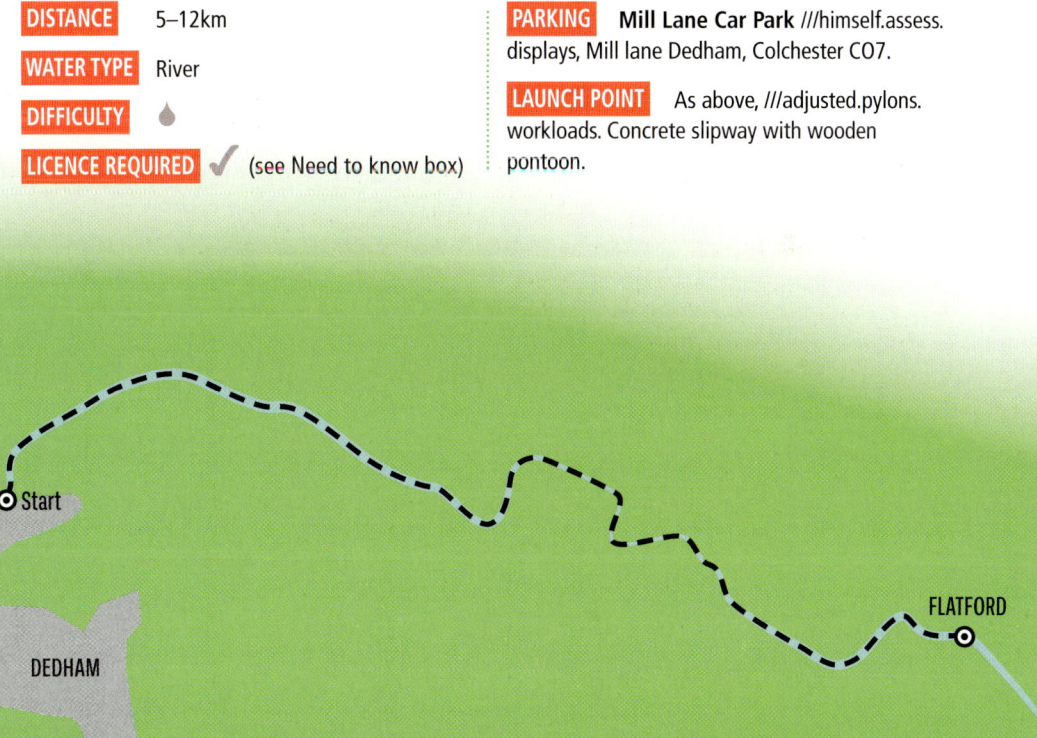

History

Dedham is in the heart of Constable county and is famed for being the place where the Romantic painter John Constable walked along the River Stour to and from school. Many of his most beloved paintings feature this beautiful stretch of river.

You are also spoilt for choice when it comes to historical architecture in Dedham, with the local church being built in the late 15th century, while the Dedham Arts Centre is set in a former church dating to 1739.

In 1705, during Queen Anne's reign, the river was widened and the 13 locks along the Stour were refurbished, making this the first navigational river in the country. Boats and barges allowed people to transport people and goods along the river. This method was eventually replaced by the railway.

Since 1986, the river has been maintained and developed by the River Stour Trust.

The paddle

Park at the Dedham Riverside car park. If it's full, Mill Lane Car Park has 127 spaces (see page 41). There's a short walk to the river across the car park, where you'll find a public launching point.

Once on the water, turn right and head downriver with the flow, under the bridge past the Boathouse (which is the pub on the riverbank). During the warmer months, this stretch of the river becomes very busy, so be mindful of hired rowing boats and other water users. The river runs alongside the Stour Valley Path, which opened in 1994 and is a 96km route from Newmarket to Cattawade.

Keep paddling until you reach Fen Bridge, a wooden bridge that was replaced in September 2023. The river will continue to wind down until you reach Flatford Mill in the little hamlet of Flatford, which was once owned by John Constable's father. Here you will find the John Constable Exhibition, which explores the life and work of the painter, along with a National Trust café, gift shop and facilities (see Food stops below). For a 5km paddle, this is your turning point, and you'll want to follow the route back upstream to Dedham.

Please note: if you would like to get off the water and visit the museum, café and facilities, please ensure you use the second portage on the right-hand side. The first portage point is private for the electric boat run by the National Trust. This offers paid trips up the river to Dedham where you have launched from.

If you decide you'd like to undertake a longer paddle, find the portage point on the right-hand side of the river, which will take you down to Cattawade, the final part of the famous Sudbury to the Sea annual event (www.riverstourtrust.org/events/s2c-basic/).

This section adds an extra 7.5km to your total paddle.

You'll pass a weir (known as Judas Gap), which is often overgrown, narrower and faster-flowing, though mostly passable. Carry on and navigate through a disused lock pool, following the river downstream, past the picnic spot and under the bridge, where you will come to the end of the non-tidal section of the Stour. At this point, turn around and retrace your route back to Dedham.

Once back at Dedham, if you want to extend this paddle further, or would like a bit of a quieter route, you can continue on into the mill pond, where you'll find a portage point on the right-hand side. Follow the portage signage up the path to the portage point, where you can continue your paddle up to Stratford St Mary and beyond.

Wildlife

On this paddle you could be treated to all sorts of wildlife, whether that be pike, grass snakes, otters, bats and a variety of birdlife, including cormorants, red kites, herons and kingfishers. And if you don't spot any wildlife, there's always the farmers' cattle!

Food stops

Dedham has plenty of food and drink stops. The Boathouse (https://theboatyardedham.co.uk), the Sun Inn (https://www.thesuninndedham.com) and the Essex Rose Tea Room (https://tiptreetearooms.com/pages/the-essex-rose) all offer a range of food and drink.

As mentioned above, there's a National Trust café at Flatford, which offers a selection of sandwiches, sausage rolls and hot and cold drinks.

A bit further down the river towards Cattawade you'll also pass Constable Park, which offers a lovely variety of food choices.

Other activities

You can hire a rowing boat or go for a nice lunch at the boathouse, visit the town or simply go for a lovely walk along the river. A short drive down the road and you'll find Hall Farm (https://hallfarmshop.com), which has a lovely café, farm trail and crazy golf.

Constable Park (https://www.constablepark.co.uk) also offers camping and glamping, which give you access to the pontoon free of charge. There is also craft hire with direct access to the river.

LEFT Aerial shot of paddleboarders at Dedham.
BELOW Aerial shot of River Stour Valley.

NEED TO KNOW

■ A Waterways Licence is required to paddle the River Stour (see page 12 for more information). This licence, available from Paddle UK or the Environment Agency, covers the entire river.

■ Be mindful of the hire rowing boats as these can cause congestion on the river.

■ Paddle distance is extendable if required.

■ Café and facilities at the turnaround point.

LEFT Dedham on a cold winters day.
BELOW Flatford Mill (National Trust).

07 RIVER COLNE

The River Colne runs from Cornish Hall End, through many Essex villages bearing its name (Colne Engaine, Earls Colne, etc) to the Colne Estuary between Brightlingsea, Point Clear and Mersea Island. Not much is navigable until you get to Colchester and towards the estuary. This paddle is in two parts – one section tidal, the other non-tidal. Part of this paddle is private – please read the Need to know box.

The Lowdown

DISTANCE Up to 13km

WATER TYPE River, tidal river towards tidal estuary

DIFFICULTY 💧 for non-tidal conditions
💧💧 for tidal

LICENCE REQUIRED ✗ (but see details for non-tidal requirement in Need to know box)

PARKING This paddle can be started from various points so there are several options for parking and launching.
FOR NON-TIDAL SECTION Colchester Canoe Club Bell Vue Road, Colchester CO1 1SH, ///laptop.lakes.entry. Club padlock securing the car park.
FOR TIDAL SECTION Rowhedge High Street, CO5 7EN, ///twig.wages.natively. Limited parking on public road and side roads next to jetty.
Wivenhoe Cooks Yard A on Walter Radcliffe Drive, CO7 9FF, ///outnumber.grows.unhappily. Small pay and display car park next to Wivenhoe Sailing Club, and again near the public jetty.
The third launch option is Hythe public jetty (below) – no parking, but for drop-off/pick-up it's a good option for a one-way paddle.

LAUNCH POINT Options depending on which section you wish to paddle:
Colchester Canoe Club ///galaxy.yours.crush
Rowhedge public jetty ///giant.speaks.payer
Wivenhoe public jetty ///nibbled.salmon.frog
Hythe public jetty ///waters.hook.urgent

History

Despite the small size of this river, it does not act as a tributary to any other river; rather, it feeds into its own estuary after passing through many Essex villages.

The main navigable non-tidal section runs through Colchester, known as the oldest recorded town (now city) and the original capital of Roman Britain. Meandering through flood plains and then Castle Park with its Norman castle still intact, this section finishes at the tidal barrier near the Old Siege House (now a bar and brasserie), famous for the bullets holes still contained in the timber frame, received during the Siege of Colchester, the 1648 battle between Royalists and Parliamentarians.

The tidal section past here runs through an area known as the Hythe, once a port area during Roman times and kept open for boats for many years by the last remaining steam dredger in the UK. However, more recently it is no longer open to commercial traffic. Now home to a few houseboats and the big red TS Colne lightship, permanently moored here and used by Colchester Sea Cadets, it is only navigable either side of high tide. From here the river winds past the villages of Rowhedge, famed in the 19th century for shipbuilding, and Wivenhoe, mentioned in the Domesday Book of 1086. Both villages were significantly damaged during the Colchester earthquake of 1884.

A tidal barrier for flood protection was built in 1994 here, past which the river continues toward the estuary.

The paddle

To paddle the non-tidal section of the Colne, launch next to the Colchester Canoe Club from a concrete path. This was a public lido in the 1930s, long since closed. Once in the river you can paddle west for a little way, under Station Way and out through Cymbeline Meadows, which act as a flood plain for the river during high water. There are only a few hundred metres of access this way before the river to too small to navigate.

The main paddle, then, is east, downstream to the left of the launch point and under Temple Bridge on Colne Bank Avenue. From here you follow the curve of the river between residential and business premises with lovely riverbanks, trees and foliage. You soon arrive at Middle Mill which, with care (in a kayak with the right safety gear) can be shot. If not, portage on the riverbank to the left and relaunch the other side of the mill via a small gate in the fence to the left of the footbridge. You'll then paddle between Castle Park, a site of historic significance (www.colchester.gov.uk/castle-park/) and the cricket ground. It can be quite shallow here and overgrown in the summer months. The river passes through Bull Meadow and past its lake, and then shortly widens again at the bottom end of the town towards the tidal barrier, which is as far as you can paddle.

BELOW Sunset view across the Colne from Wivenhoe to Rowhedge.

ABOVE View of the Sea Cadet Lightship from the river.

During the height of summer this non-tidal section can be very weedy, particularly at the club end, making for a difficult paddle.

For the second part of this paddle – the tidal section of the river – there are three options to launch. All three are best an hour or two before high tide so that you're paddling in with the rising tide and back out with the falling tide. All three launches allow you to paddle into Colchester and the tidal side of the barrier at the end of the non-tidal paddle described above.

If you have parked at either Rowhedge or Wivenhoe, the paddle is the same, but you need to paddle to the left at Rowhedge, or to the right at Wivenhoe to get you into Colchester.

You can also paddle carefully out through the Colne Tide Barrier against the tide and immediately to the right is a small tributary to the Colne called the Roman River. This is quite small and very tidal but can add a little interest to your day.

Paddling into Colchester from either of the launch points sees you follow the Wivenhoe Trail and the railway line along the river. Passing Wivenhoe Woods and Lower Lodge Farms nature reserves on your right and the salt marsh moorings on your left, you soon leave the villages and head toward Colchester.

The area on your left is now farmland

and home to the Hythe Lagoons, situated just before you arrive in the Hythe area of Colchester. As you paddle past the old port area there are houseboats and a lightship opposite the large tower blocks of student accommodation for Essex University (the Hythe public pontoon is also located here, if you're after a shorter, alternative launch).

The river now starts to narrow, with more vegetation either side as you work towards the end of the tidal section, and once under East Street with the Siege House and the old mills on your right, you're as far as you can go – around 6km from Rowhedge each way. If you have timed the tide well you will soon paddle back to your launch by retracing your steps (or strokes!).

Wildlife

The launch area at Colchester Canoe Club is home to a family of swans who regularly breed and bring up their young in the reeds. Note, they can be very protective.

As with any tidal river you will see many types of seabirds, and with the nature reserves along the way you may also spot birds of prey hunting. The Colne Estuary is home to seals and porpoises – they will probably not wander this far upriver, but you may get lucky.

Food stops

Both Rowhedge and Wivenhoe have a good choice of pubs and coffee shops near to the river.

In Rowhedge, Ye Olde Albion pub and The Anchor are right next to the river, while 'The Hut' at the local rowing club is open during the summer for tea, coffee and cake. Also worthy of mention is the nearby Jam Jar, which serves locally sourced speciality tea and coffee.

In Wivenhoe, there's the Rose and Crown and The Black Buoy a short walk from the car park.

Colchester City Centre is a short walk from the Canoe Club, with lots of bars and restaurants available.

Other activities

As the oldest recorded town in Britain, Colchester has a lot to see, from the Norman castle, built around 1076, to the Roman wall (including where Humpty Dumpty apparently fell), and the Natural History Museum, all of which can be found in the City Centre.

If you want to walk or cycle along the route we paddle, the Wivenhoe Trail runs along the river from Castle Park (see above) to Wivenhoe. Or the public ferry can give you a lift to Rowhedge, and from there you could walk back along the other side of the river. From Wivenhoe you can also continue along a public footpath all the way to Alresford and Brightlingsea.

NEED TO KNOW

■ As there is no portage between the tidal and non-tidal sections of the River Colne, and due to access restrictions and the tidal nature of the river, this paddle is divided into two parts: non-tidal and tidal. No licence is required for either (see page 12), but the non-tidal section of the river can only be accessed at Colchester Canoe Club and to do so you must be a member of the club, or the guest of a member. This is because Colchester Borough Council owns the riparian rights of the riverbank and its surroundings.

■ The Canoe Club has managed to gain an exclusive licence for its use from the council. Club membership at time of writing is £30 for the year for adults. More details can be found here: https://colchestercanoeclub.co.uk/.

08 OSEA ISLAND

Osea Island is a small private island east of Heybridge Basin in the Blackwater Estuary. This paddle is dependent on high tide to coincide with the halfway point of the paddle around the west end of the island. There are very few public launch points around the estuary suitable for this paddle, and for this reason it is best completed from Stone Sailing Club (see Need to know box for more details).

The Lowdown

- **DISTANCE** 10km
- **WATER TYPE** Tidal estuary
- **DIFFICULTY**
- **LICENCE REQUIRED** ✗ (but limited access – see Need to know box) Only available to members of Stone Sailing Club (see Need to know box)
- **PARKING** Only available to members of Stone Sailing Club (see Need to know box)
- **LAUNCH POINT** On the beach at Stone Sailing Club, Tinnocks Lane, St Lawrence, Southminster CM0 7NF, ///lyricist.kilowatt.tycoons.

History

Osea Island has a long and varied history, being settled in Neolithic times and used for Viking burials. It is private and can only be accessed by a causeway at low tide, which was built by the Romans who occupied and settled on the island. Ownership has changed hands throughout the centuries, and it was often passed down through families during Tudor times. During the war the island became a secret base for motor torpedo boats, while in more recent years it has played host to wellness retreats and film crews. Top music producer Nigel Frieda, mentor to The Rolling Stones and Roxy Music, has owned the island since 2004, and it is now a retreat for musicians, such as pop star Rihanna, who come here for the world-class recording studios, luxury resort and peaceful rural atmosphere.

OSEA ISLAND

Start and finish

ABOVE Flamingo-shaped beach from the air.

The Blackwater Estuary, in which Osea Island is located, is between Maldon and West Mersea. Areas of the estuary are variously designated a biological Site of Special Scientific Interest, a Ramsar Wetland of International Importance, a Special Protection Area and a National Nature Reserve, being home to many species of bird and waterfowl. Oysters have been farmed in these tidal waters since Anglo-Saxon times over 1,000 years ago.

The estuary is tidal and is the exit of the River Blackwater and Chelmer, leading out to the East Coast and North Sea.

The paddle

As you launch from the beach at the sailing club, Osea Island is to your west. This paddle is described as leaving the island to the right and heading clockwise around it to the south and then north of the island.

Leaving the beach and paddling along the shoreline with the incoming tide, you soon reach Marconi Sailing Club, formed in the 1950s by employees of the Marconi Wireless Telegraph Company Limited on the Stansgate Peninsula. As you paddle further it is worth looking back over your shoulder to see Stansgate House, former home of the Labour MP Tony Benn.

You are now paddling in the River Blackwater channel as you head over towards the island. Note, you cannot land on any part of the island at this point, due to its status as a wildlife haven and it being a private retreat.

Continue to the west, past a few piers to the most westerly point of the island, and if you've time it right it should now be high tide. You should be able to spot many of the cottages and apartments on the island that are available to book. This end of Osea is also a great spot to watch the sunset.

Paddling back towards the launch point with the outgoing tide, you're now on the north of Osea, between the island and the beautiful village of Goldhanger in Goldhanger Creek. At this point you will paddle over the ancient Roman causeway, which is the only access to the island for four hours each day. Staying close to the island, continue along its shoreline and as you get to the most easterly point, you'll come to a small beach, the only place the public can land. From the air it looks like a flamingo's head, a gentle, sloping stone beach with a small lagoon to land and have a picnic.

From here it's a short paddle back across the River Blackwater to Stone Sailing Club and the end of the paddle. On the return leg you can clearly see Bradwell Power Station, a Magnox-design nuclear power station which, since 1984, has been undergoing decommissioning, the first of its type to do so in the UK. If you have a clear day and can see into the distance you may even spot MV *Ross Revenge*, a bright red-painted ship that between 1983 and 1990 was home to pirate radio station Radio Caroline.

Wildlife

The estuary is a waterfowl paradise, with a mixture of habitats including marshland, mudflats, lagoons, offshore islands and disused gravel pits. Areas of the estuary are variously designated a biological Site of Special Scientific Interest, a Ramsar Wetland of International Importance, a Special Protection Area and a National Nature Reserve. Overwintering species include pied avocet, dunlin, Eurasian golden plover, dark-bellied brent goose, black-tailed godwit, and many more. It's also a breeding site for little tern and a transit point for ringed plover.

Food stops

There are limited options on this paddle to stop and eat, so we recommend taking a picnic. However, you can grab a bite to eat on the way home at one of the various pubs and restaurants in the nearby area, or from the Sailing Club Galley (see Need to know box).

Other activities

This sparsely populated area is also a walking and cycling paradise. The Dengie Peninsula is close by, where you'll find the National Nature Reserve, country parks and the famous Chapel of St Peter-on-the-Wall, originally constructed as an Anglo-Celtic church for the East Saxons in AD 654 by St Cedd, astride the ruins of the abandoned Roman fort of Othona.

NEED TO KNOW

- Parking and launching is only available to members of Stone Sailing Club (www.stonesc.org.uk/) or as part of an annual paddling event organised by the sailing club in conjunction with East of England Paddlesports.

- As this is a tidal section of the Blackwater Estuary, you don't require a licence to paddle, but timing is critical for launch (see page 12 for more information).

- This paddle is around 10km and completed in two to three hours, particularly if you use the tide and the wind is light. Plan for a longer trip if the wind is strong or conditions a little choppy. Ideally, aim to launch around one to two hours before high tide.

- Whether you paddle clockwise or anticlockwise around the island, leaving the island to your right or left, will depend on the wind direction. You are aiming to gain the most shelter from the wind.

09 TWO TREE ISLAND TO MULBERRY HARBOUR

Two Tree Island is a small island next to Canvey Island, connected to the mainland at Leigh in Essex by a single-span road bridge. The island is now home to a 257-hectare nature reserve, which sits adjacent to the Thames Estuary, where the River Thames meets the waters of the North Sea. Access to the water here is possible via the slipway at all times of the tide. The slipway can be slippery, so be sure to take care when launching during lower tide states. With the river being tidal and fast-flowing, a good understanding of tide times and currents is essential, as well as researching certain channels to navigate, as not all lead out to the sea at low tide!

The Lowdown

DISTANCE 22km
WATER TYPE Tidal
DIFFICULTY ●●●
LICENCE REQUIRED ✗
PARKING Two Tree Island Nature Reserve High Street, Castle Point District, Southend-on-Sea, SS9 2GB, ///frosted.adults.fade. Free.

LAUNCH POINT Slipway ///error.rocks.volume. Launch fees for all craft using the slipway. Head out on to the long slipway in the main car park. Be mindful as it can be quite slippery.

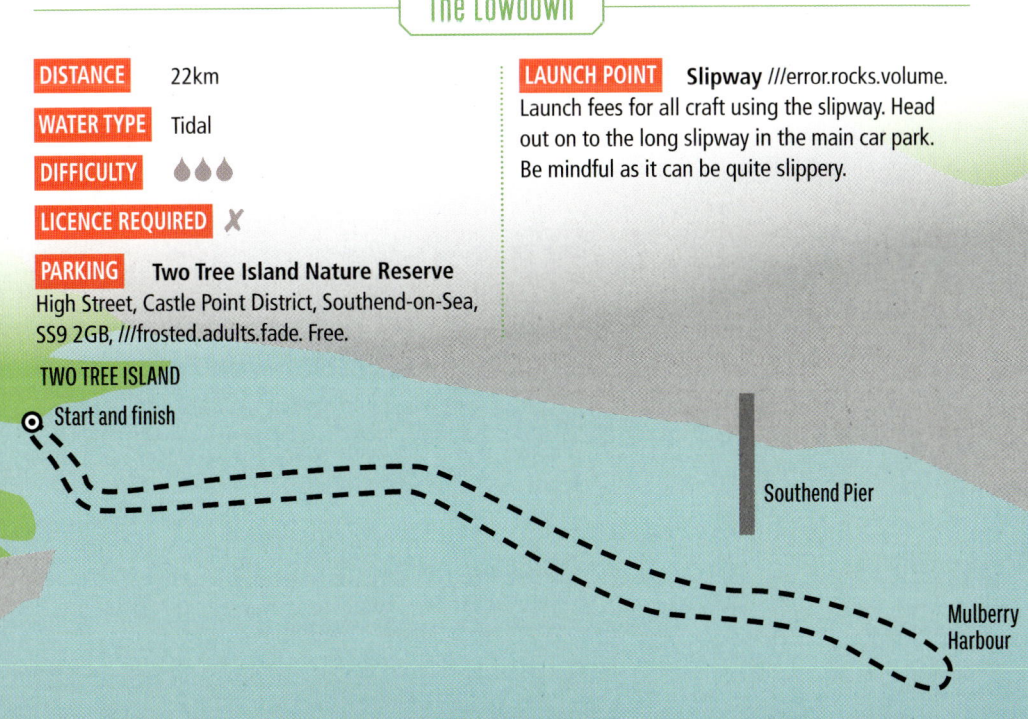

TWO TREE ISLAND
Start and finish

Southend Pier

Mulberry Harbour

History

The name 'Two Tree Island' comes from two large elm trees that were a prominent feature on the island until they were brought down by storms in the early 1960s.

In the 18th century, when the land was reclaimed from the sea, a seawall was built, creating Two Tree Island, which was then mostly used for farmland and grazing animals – this happened up until 1910, when a sewage works was built on part of the island. This remained in operation for a large part of the 20th century. Adding another chapter to its industrial use, the entire island became a landfill site in 1936, running until 1974, when it was shut down and the area eventually re-seeded, allowing nature to take over.

Today, Two Tree Island is a haven for wildlife and a popular nature reserve managed by the Essex Wildlife Trust.

The paddle

For this paddle it's worth heading out around 2.5 hours before low tide, aiming to get the Mulberry Harbour wreck just before the low water time to be able to get out on the sand and walk around and swim. When leaving the slip at Two Tree Island, look backwards and take a moment to familiarise yourself with the landmarks, particularly Hadleigh Castle and the Benfleet water tower on the skyline, as the car park won't be so obvious on the way back! You want to paddle out and follow the main channel of Hadleigh Ray creek. You'll see three possible creeks: the first two almost directly in front of you, and then the main channel heading towards the chimneys and cranes in Kent. As you paddle out, this takes an almost 90 degree to the right, heading south. This is the channel that you need to take as the first two channels end in mud (if you get it wrong, it will become quite obvious, as you won't be able to go anywhere!) This main channel will also eventually be marked with navigation bouys, which you can follow out and in!

Before you get there, you will paddle past lots of banks, where you'll often see seals lounging around. When you get close to the pier be mindful of the conditions; it can be quite rough and you wouldn't want to find yourself being pushed under the pier. Your best bet is to paddle around the outside, while on your return journey you can paddle

ABOVE Seals basking on the mudflat.
LEFT Paddling towards Southend Pier.

under clearer sections of the pier walkway if you wish. Fishermen often fish for mackerel, plaice and flounder off the end of the pier, so be mindful of lines in the water. The RNLI has a station here, too.

Southend Pier is famous for being the world's longest pleasure pier, stretching 2.16km into the Thames Estuary! It was also the first pier to have a railway installed. On another day, you can enjoy the pier, arcades and restaurants from above, but paddling past it you'll get an impressive view of the structure, and one not many people get to see. In the distance, you'll spot the Mulberry Harbour; you're still about 3.2km from reaching it, so keep paddling!

The remains of the harbour aren't complete, but they're a fascinating piece of war history. The huge concrete structure you see in the water up ahead is known as a Phoenix caisson, just one piece of the much larger Mulberry harbours, two temporary portable harbours developed during the Second World War to facilitate the rapid offloading of reinforcements and supplies onto beaches during the Allied invasion of Normandy in June 1944. Roughly 130 were built in secret around the UK, and then sunk, ready to be retrieved and towed across the English Channel when needed. This piece of the Mulberry Harbour never made it to France; while towing out it developed a leak, so was sunk here. It now sits on a sandy bank, and has split in half due to the uneven ground. You can get a close-up look at the impressive work that went into creating these structures, including all the steel cables used to reinforce the concrete.

As the water starts to return, you need to think about your return journey. An easy marker point from here is the pier. Depending on conditions, head for the walkway and paddle under. You are literally

ABOVE The Mulberry Harbour.

following your route back, but it can be harder to spot where you need to head. So, follow the main land, back towards Canvey Island, and you'll spot Hadleigh Castle in the distance. Once you're in front of Canvey, turn to the right, and then left, where you should begin to see the slipway. Keep your eyes peeled for the RNLI marker buoys in the channel – if you stick close to those, you should be able to follow them back and make it home without any issues.

Wildlife Two Tree Island nature reserve boasts a huge variety of habitats, including mudflats, saltmarshes and scrubland. You are very likely to see lots of birdlife, ranging from year-round visitors such as little grebe, grey heron, little egret, sparrowhawk and kestrel, to spring and winter visitors including nightingale, chiffchaff, brent goose and curlew. A more comprehensive list can be found on the Essex Birdwatching Society website (https://www.ebws.org.uk).

While on the water, it is very common to see lots of grey seals basking on the warm mudflats, or even following you on your paddle! It is, of course, important to respect the sea life you encounter, and give them a wide, quiet birth so as not to spook them. Never try to touch or feed the seals.

Food stops Due to the nature of this paddle, there are no facilities. Instead, we recommend bringing your own packed lunch, snacks and drinks. After your paddle, head into Southend, which hosts an array of eateries.

Other activities There is so much to do in this area, including great walks, cycling and sightseeing. Hadleigh Castle is nearby, the pier is worth a visit and there's Adventure Island for the kids, a small theme park at the entrance to the pier.

To see the Mulberry Harbour, you can walk out from Thorpe Bay. Be sure to go at low tide and be careful on mud flats, when you'll often see people swimming around the pools created at the base of the Phoenix caisson. Be sure to check tide times, as you don't want to be caught out here when the water returns!

NEED TO KNOW

■ To complete this paddle, in order to be able to get out and walk around the Mulberry Harbour, you need to plan your journey around the tide times, aiming to be at the harbour for low tide. As this is a tidal area, you don't require a licence to paddle (see page 12 for more information).

■ Ensure you check the wind speed and direction.

■ Always paddle within your capabilities.

10 MERSEA ISLAND TO TOLLESBURY

Mersea Island sits in the Blackwater and Colne estuaries to the south of Colchester. Lots of paddle routes are available from Mersea; however being tidal, you'll need to have an understanding of the tides before setting out. Saying that, being an estuary, this is a fairly safe area to paddle, with access to the water at high and low tide – so expect to see lots of kayakers, paddleboarders and rowers here. Footwear is advised at all times due to the nature of the ground: a mix of rocks, mud and sand – with lots of sharp oyster shells.

The Lowdown

DISTANCE 10km
WATER TYPE Tidal
DIFFICULTY ●●
LICENCE REQUIRED ✗

PARKING **Coast Road car park**
115 Coast Road, West Mersea CO5 8PA, ///anyway.relatives.forge. Pay and display at time of writing. Toilet facilities. Roughly 28 spaces (side-road parking can be found heading further inland – please check limitations).

LAUNCH POINT ///fancy.kings.regarding. Seen from Coast Road car park. At low tide be sure to stay within the hard ground, as either side gets muddy!

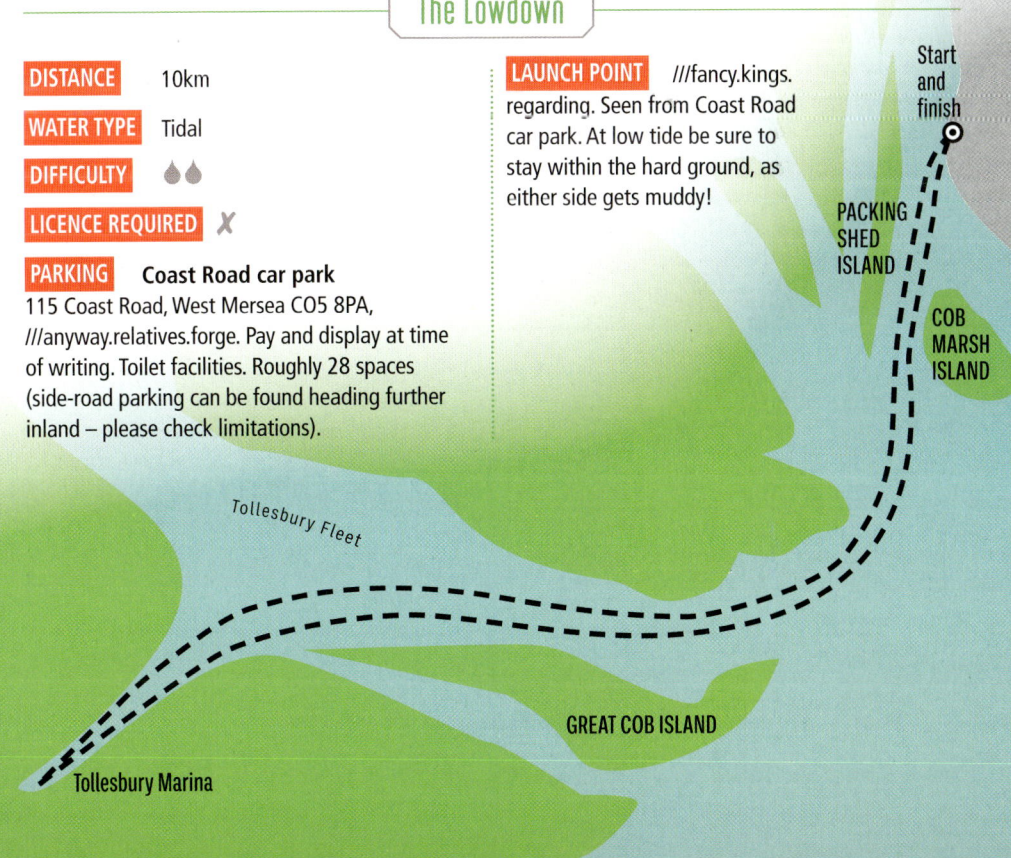

History

Mersea's name comes from the Old English word *Meresig*, meaning 'island of the pool'. Mersea Island is the most easterly inhabited island in Britain. The island is split into two main areas, West and East Mersea, and is connected to the mainland by the Strood, a causeway that can flood at high tide – making Mersea a true island. The harbour in West Mersea is used by fishing vessels year-round, producing lots of fresh produce, including world-famous oysters!

The paddle

From the car park, you'll see the boat launch area. From here, you can paddle past the Packing Shed Island, on either side, taking note of the channel markers and any moving traffic. Ahead of you is Bradwell Power Station, which sits on the Dengie Peninsula at the mouth of the River Blackwater, before it merges with the North Sea.

Once you reach the mouth of the channel, you'll be turning right, hugging the land as you go. You'll paddle past the Old Hall Marshes Nature Reserve, which is an area of mudflats and salt marshes, where often you'll be able to spot plenty of birdlife. Ensuring you turn right into the first channel, you'll start to enter into the creeks. You'll paddle past Great Cob Island – be

RIGHT Boat wreck in Tollesbury.
BELOW Aerial view of the Tollesbury Lightship.

sure to keep either side of the mainland and Cob Island, as it will be shallow nearer the land – you don't want to beach yourself! The turning into Tollesbury is to your left, into Woodrolfe Creek. You'll see a sign welcoming you into Tollesbury Marina – continue along here, where you'll pass a big red lightship owned by Fellowship Afloat Charitable Trust (FACT), which offers outdoor education and courses (www.fact.org.uk/).

Keep paddling and you'll wind your way past several little boat wrecks and marshes, to the harbour. The best place to head for is the big wooden shed, which is part of the marina. Depending on tides, you should be able to paddle up the slipway on to the road, where you can get out and leave your kit up by the wall. Be mindful of the rising tide; you don't want your craft to float away! From here you can walk up into the village to find refreshments, while on your left you'll see the Woodup community pool, a salt water bathing area with a picnic area, BBQs and toilets – a nice place to pause.

Retrace this route for your homeward journey, making this paddle just under 10km long. If you plan to arrive in Tollesbury for high tide, you'll have the easier conditions on your paddle. When you launch, you'll be going against the incoming tide until you turn right, where you'll be pushed along all the way into Tollesbury. Ride the outgoing tide and you'll be pushed along until you head back in towards Mersea, where you'll have a bit of outgoing tide to contend with.

Wildlife

There is always a good chance of spotting wildlife around here, and an abundance of birdlife exists, with lots of nesting land in the vicinity. Sometimes you'll be able to spot seals and, on very rare occasions, even porpoises can be seen in the main channel. Paddling close to Tollesbury Wick offers a better chance for birdlife, including various species of geese and marsh harriers.

Food stops

In Tollesbury you'll find several places offering good, hearty food. The local sailing club has an open restaurant and The Loft and Tollesbury Café are both really good and well suited to walk to for a snack.

From Mersea, right behind the car park you'll find the Blackwater Pearl café. Just along from the café is the Coast Inn, and a little further along you'll find The Victory pub. All serve great food and drinks, and there's plenty of outdoor seating available.

Other activities

In Tollesbury there are so many walking options – around the Old Hall Marshes Nature Reserve and Tollesbury Wick, and the local sailing clubs. Mersea has several popular walking options and providers offering boat trips around the local area.

TOP Tollesbury Marina boat shed.
BOTTOM Woodup Salt Pool.

NEED TO KNOW

- As this is a tidal section of the Colne Estuary, you don't require a licence to paddle, but timing is critical for launch (see page 12 for more information).
- Check tide times and heights to ensure plenty of water to complete the paddle.
- Tollesbury is not accessible from the water at low tide. Be sure to leave with the outgoing tide, which will help your return paddle to Mersea.
- There are no nearby public facilities in Tollesbury.

11 MALDON LOOP

Maldon is a historic maritime and market town situated at the head of the Blackwater Estuary, and one of the oldest recorded towns in Essex. The River Chelmer flows entirely through the county of Essex, around 64km from the north-west of the county through Chelmsford to the River Blackwater, near Maldon. There are a few popular spots along the river to paddle, though we have chosen to focus on Heybridge Basin, which is a great starting point (with parking) from which to paddle this loop. You need to have a good understanding of tide times to make this paddle work, and you should launch an hour or two before high tide. This stretch of water, known as the Chelmer and Blackwater Navigation, is managed by Essex Waterways.

The Lowdown

DISTANCE 10km

WATER TYPE Tidal/river

DIFFICULTY

LICENCE REQUIRED (see Need to know box)

PARKING Daisy Meadow Maldon CM9 4RW, ///ordinary.notebook.structure. Pay and display at time of writing. Approx. 130 spaces.

LAUNCH POINT Ideally, launch around 2 hr before high water to complete the loop. A short walk from the car park, up some stairs, brings you to the Chelmer & Blackwater Navigation Canal. You can paddle this anytime. ///declares.irrigate.distract

History

Maldon's story is deeply linked to the River Blackwater. People have lived along this river since the Iron Age. The Anglo-Saxons called it Maeldun, meaning 'monument on the hill', and built a significant port here to facilitate fishing and trade. Vikings also sailed the Blackwater, and battled the Anglo-Saxons, led by Earl Byrhtnoth, here at the Battle of Maldon in AD 991. A statue of Byrhtnoth, who was killed in the battle, can be seen in Maldon, overlooking the estuary.

Maldon was granted a Royal Charter by Henry II in 1171, in part to due to its strategic importance alongside the river. The people of Maldon used the Blackwater for trade, but faced struggles with the Crown over rights. Despite this, the river kept the town alive and today Maldon retains its charm. You'll find historic buildings, a bustling quayside and, of course, the famous Maldon Sea Salt, harvested from the river's bounty. Its production dates back to Roman times.

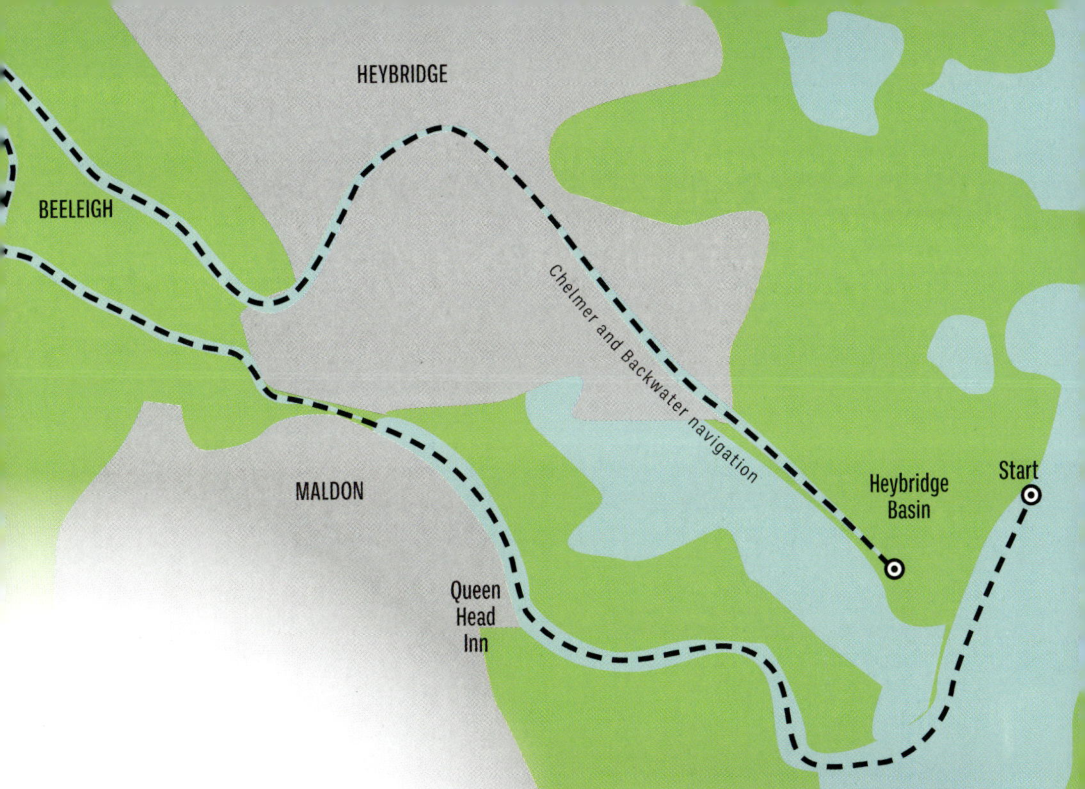

The paddle

Ideally, you would launch around two hours before high water to complete the loop. A short walk from the car park, up some stairs brings you to the Chelmer and Blackwater Navigation canal. Turn left and walk along the canal bank to the sea wall. If the water is high enough you can launch here. If not, walk along the sea wall to the left (between the Jolly Sailor Pub and the Lock Tea Room) for approximately five minutes and you will find a small beach. This is our preferred launch point.

Once you've launched, paddle towards the right, passing between Heybridge Basin and Northey Island. This is the tidal section, where the River Blackwater and the River Chelmer meet. Conditions here can be quite rough, so be sure to check wind forecasts before you set off. Follow the river round to the right, entering into the smaller section of the river, passing Herrings Point, a small nature reserve. You're now passing the

ABOVE Ready to launch.

Maldon Promenade Park. You'll see the statue of Byrhtnoth, standing proud on the tip of the sea wall.

Continue on, passing the park, then Maldon Splash Park, Maldon Marine Lake and the harbour. A good resting spot is the Queen's Head Inn – easy access is available here, though be sure not to block any access with your kit. You'll want to make sure you have plenty of time to carry on riding the flow of the tide, to get to the ancient hamlet of Beeleigh. Before getting there though, you need to paddle under Fullbridge, a road which crosses the River Chelmer. On higher tides there is very little space between the bridge and the water, which can be a little risky, so please be very careful as you paddle beneath it!

You'll now paddle under the A414 road bridge. Keep going, taking in the sights around you. Just before the bridge, on the right is a piece of land called the Chelmer Blackwater Reserve Community Interest Company – 'Ironworks Meadow'. This land has been saved from development and the community aims to manage and improve it as a wildlife reserve with public access, including a boardwalk. Keep your eyes peeled for wildlife around here!

As you continue, you'll hear the sounds from the Beeleigh Falls get louder. This isn't your typical waterfall; it's a hidden gem with a surprising amount of intrigue. It's actually a series of weirs and locks built in the 1790s – not for dramatic views, but a practical purpose: allowing horse-drawn barges to navigate the Chelmer and Blackwater Navigation. Moreover, the falls isn't just one body of water cascading down – it's a confluence! Here, the River Chelmer, River Blackwater, the Chelmer & Blackwater Navigation Canal and the tidal River Chelmer all meet, creating a unique aquatic junction. The town of Maldon wasn't a fan of the canal, so the builders had to get creative. The Beeleigh Falls section was actually dug by hand to bypass Maldon entirely and connect to Heybridge Basin on the Blackwater Estuary. Talk about perseverance!

You need to get out at this point. There are two options: towards the falls on the right is a bit of land, which is closest to your next get-in but can be muddy. To the left of the bridge there is another option – get out here and carry your kit across the

bridge, making your way to the Chelmer and Blackwater Navigation section, just past the huge lock. Again, this is another nice spot to pause and take a break. There's a road here, though, so be mindful of moving traffic. From here the paddle back to Daisy Meadow is relatively straightforward. You'll pass by Maldon Golf Club on your right, under the Elms Farm Park Bridge, past a big Tesco supermarket, lots of offices and industrial

TOP Brytnoth standing proud.

LEFT Pit stop at the Queens Head.

RIGHT Floating under the road bridge.

units, and then a long straight section gets you back to the car park. Keep your eyes peeled for terrapins here, usually seen basking in the sunshine on a floating log or the river bank.

Food stops

There are several options for sustenance around this paddle location. Your starting point has the Daisy Meadow Kiosk (CM9 4RY, ///parkland.slime.yappy), which offers light lunches, drinks and snacks. Bear in mind that depending when you launch, this could be closed on your return! There are several pubs by the Basin Lock (where the paddle starts): The Old Ship (a favourite to sit out after the paddle) and

ABOVE Paddling towards the Elms Farm Park Bridge.

The Jolly Sailor. There is also the Lock Tea Room.

As mentioned above, the Queen's Head Inn is a great spot to pause mid-paddle. You can even use the portage by the Tesco supermarket to get out and make use of the facilities or purchase snacks. I like to pack my own lunch for a break at the Beeleigh Lock, once you're off the tidal section, as it's far less reliant on timing.

Wildlife

Kestrels raise their young along the river. You're also likely to catch a glimpse of oystercatchers, swans, ducks and, if you're lucky, woodpeckers, owls and cuckoos. A large range of fish can be found here, usually chub, carp, bream, perch, pike, roach, rudd, dace, brown and rainbow trout – with this many options you're bound to pass a friendly fisherman or two. On warm, sunny days you might even be lucky enough to spot a terrapin basking in the sunshine. And, while they may not be real, as you launch, be sure to check surrounding gardens for a huge display of really wild wildlife, including gorillas, giraffes and elephants!

Other activities

There are plenty of walks around the area, following along the waterways. Maldon is a lovely spot, where you can find lots of shops and entertainment. Promenade Park is a great place for the family, with water splash parks, model boat lakes, parks and café's. See Visit Maldon's website for more information: www.visitmaldondistrict.co.uk.

NEED TO KNOW

- Paddlers must pay for a licence before launching. Day or annual licences can be purchased online at www.waterways.org.uk, or in Heybridge at the Daisy Meadow Kiosk (CM9 4RY, ///parkland.slime.yappy) during opening hours (see page 12 for more information).

- To complete the loop you need to plan around the tide times. Ensure you check the wind speed and direction, too.

- Always paddle within your capabilities.

12 MULBERRY HARBOUR AND SOUTHEND PIER

Located in the Thames Estuary in the south-east of Essex, these famous feats of engineering – both recognised as historic landmarks – can be combined into one trip, or paddled separately from various locations. We have chosen to start and finish the paddle in Thorpe Bay.

The Lowdown

DISTANCE 5–10km
WATER TYPE Tidal estuary
DIFFICULTY 💧💧
LICENCE REQUIRED ✗

PARKING **The Broadway** Southend-on-Sea SS1 3HL, ///along.skin.choice. Side roads. Free, avoiding yellow lines.
Thorpe Esplanade Southend-on-Sea SS1 3NN, ///life.skin.voters. Either directly on road or in pay and display car park (height barrier 2.1m).

LAUNCH POINT SS1 3HL, ///option.rent.shirt. Launch from the sand/stone beach between breakwaters, accessed from the car parks along the main esplanade and down steps.

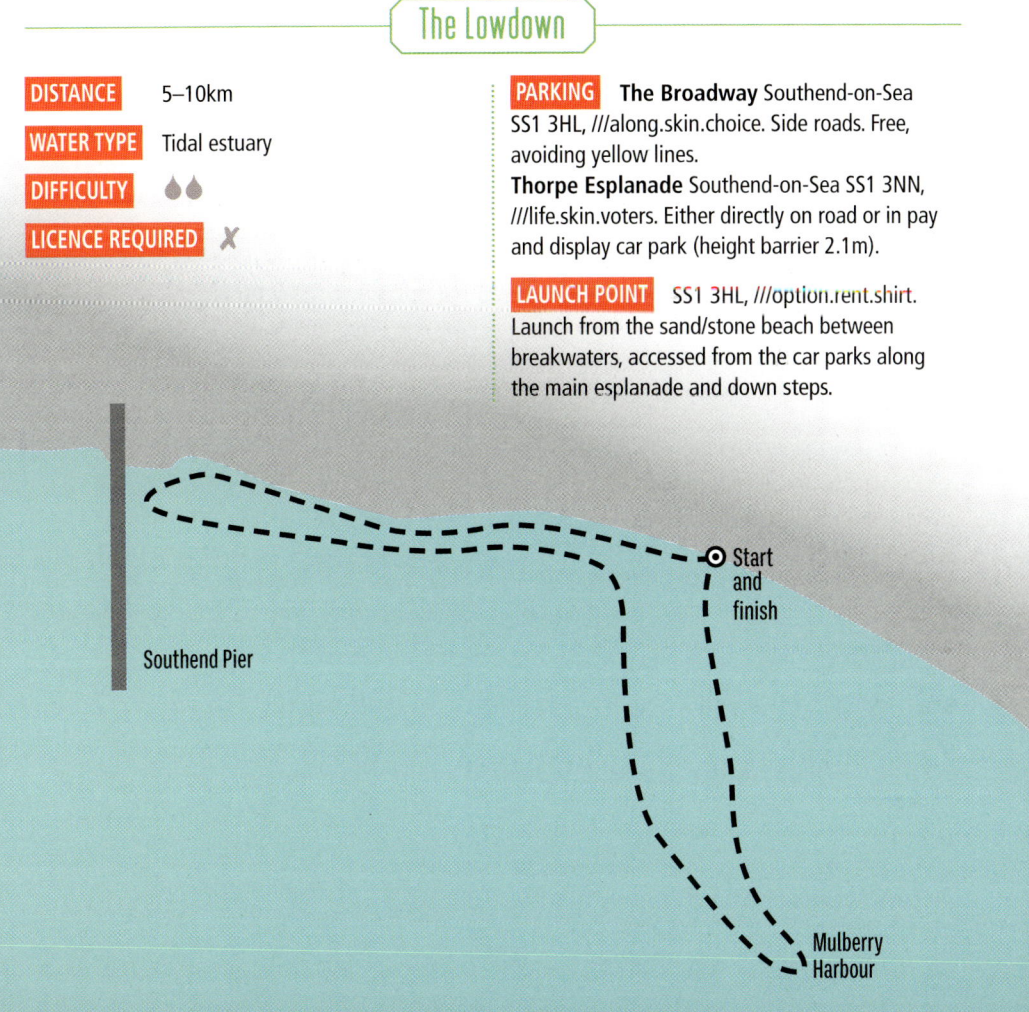

History

While referred to by many as the Mulberry Harbour, this landmark is actually one of the wartime concrete caissons built as temporary harbours to be used as a resupply base during the D-Day landings in Normandy. The caissons are concrete and were designed to float and be towed to France, then scuttled near the landing beaches to form breakwaters. The section you see here was designated a scheduled monument in 2004. It sprung a leak on its journey to France, from where it was built in Immingham, and was towed into the Thames Estuary and left to sink. It is now in two parts, having broken its back, located on Knock Sands almost 2km south–south-west from Shoeburyness. While it is possible to walk to the caisson at low tide, it is advised only to do so with a local guide, as the sandbanks and mudflats are notorious for stranding people.

Southend Pier was built in various guises from the early to late 1800s. Its current form – reaching 2km out across the sand and mudflats to meet the main shipping channel – was constructed and then extended in the late 1890s, making it the longest pleasure pier in the world. Since then, it has burnt down, been cut in half by ships and generally had a hard life. Today, though, it is a fixture of the British seaside, home to amusements, cafés and a narrow gauge railway service, which runs every half hour from end to end.

The paddle

You can see the Mulberry Harbour from the beach around 2km roughly

RIGHT The view looking in toward the beach.

BELOW A sunrise view the Harbour from the beach side with the shipping marker on top; the section to the left sloping down is the smaller section.

south of the launch point. Bearing in mind the incoming tide will push you towards the west, you will need to track a little to the east to stay on target. Once at the harbour, and depending on the height of the tide, you should clearly see the two concrete sections and be able to paddle around and through them, subject to conditions. They're often slick with seaweed and also home to shellfish, so landing on them to walk around is not advised.

From the Harbour to Southend Pier, paddle to the west with the tide (assuming you have launched as above). Again, you can see the pier in the distance, which is just under 3km away. The route shown on the accompanying map has you paddling back in towards and then along the beach to the land end of the pier, although you can of course head for the end of the pier, but that depends on conditions. Also, do remember that this is a shipping lane up to Tilbury Port, Dartford and London.

Once at the pier you can see people strolling along it, the trains ferrying people to the end and back, and the amusements in full swing along the promenade.

If you have timed your paddle well the journey back is a nice, easy paddle along the beach with the tide as it goes out back to your launch point. Obviously this is beach all the way, so a picnic stop is certainly a great addition – just watch the tide and don't get stuck in the mud.

Wildlife

Depending on how clear the water is you may see fish. Seals frequent the sand banks at low tide, basking in the sunshine. There is an abundance of seabirds, including various species of gull, oystercatchers, avocets and black-tailed godwits. Check out the website for the Port of London Authority for more

information: https://pla.co.uk/nature-biodiversity#ecology.

If you're very lucky you may even spot a harbour porpoise, which, although very shy, are believed to use the estuary as a nursery.

Food stops

Since you're close to the seaside resort town of Southend-on-Sea, you're in a prime location for fish and chips, seafood and shellfish. You can either stop during your paddle near the pier or take a nice walk from your parking spot after your paddle.

Other activities

Southend-on-Sea has been a popular holiday destination since Victorian times, and you'll find all the usual seaside fare, including amusements arcades and shopping. There is also now a large fun fair with rides for all the family. For the quieter life, staying near to the suggested launch point you'll find lots of cafés and tea shops for a nice post-paddle cuppa or ice cream.

NEED TO KNOW

■ As this is a tidal section of the Thames Estuary, you don't require a licence to paddle, but timing is critical for launch (see page 12 for more information). Plan to launch between one and two hours before high tide, as when the tide is out the sticky mudflats are exposed.

■ This paddle is around 10km and completed in two to three hours, particularly if you use the tide and the wind is light. Plan for a longer trip if the wind is strong or conditions a little choppy.

■ The main shipping lane to the Port of Tilbury is in the middle of the estuary, although you are unlikely to get close to it during this paddle.

BELOW Looking out to sea and the shipping channel. You can clearly see the iron structure from 1889 some of which is still original.

13 MERSEA ISLAND TO THE STROOD

Mersea Island sits in the Blackwater and Colne estuaries to the south of Colchester. Lots of paddle routes are available from Mersea; however being tidal, you'll need to have an understanding of the tides before setting out. Saying that, being an estuary, this is a fairly safe area to paddle, with access to the water at high and low tide – so expect to see lots of kayakers, paddleboarders and rowers here. Footwear is advised at all times due to the nature of the ground: a mix of rocks, mud and sand – with lots of sharp oyster shells.

The Lowdown

DISTANCE 6km
WATER TYPE Tidal
DIFFICULTY ●●
LICENCE REQUIRED ✗
PARKING **Coast Road car park** 115 Coast Road, West Mersea CO5 8PA, ///anyway.relatives.forge. Pay and display at time of writing. Toilet facilities. Roughly 28 spaces (side-road parking can be found heading further inland – please check limitations).

LAUNCH POINT ///fancy.kings.regarding. Looking out to the water, there's a boat slip to your left.

History

Mersea's name comes from the Old English word *Meresig*, meaning 'island of the pool'. Mersea Island is the most easterly inhabited island in Britain. The island is split into two main areas, West and East Mersea, and is connected to the mainland by the Strood, a causeway that can flood at high tide – making Mersea a true island. The harbour in West Mersea is used by fishing vessels year-round, producing lots of fresh produce, including world-famous oysters!

The paddle

From the car park, looking out to the water, on your left you will see the boat launch. It's worth noting that there's a hard path that leads from the launch area, out to the right, following a curved line towards two wooden posts. (Interesting fact: on the left post there is a white painted line. This marks the level the water needs to be at for it to be covering the Strood!)

Once launched, you can head out towards the right.

A nice little addition would be to paddle to the left, towards Packing Shed Island – a small island with a black wooden hut (The Packing Shed), built in the 1890s as a place to help manage the growing oyster trade. They would clean and pack the oysters here, before sending them off to nearby towns, London and eventually around the world. When production outgrew this small set-up, the shed became more of a museum, and is now available to hire as a wedding and party venue. It is also a very popular nesting site, so be sure to check any signage before stopping.

Paddle past the hammerhead jetty (back towards where you started if you took the extra additional paddle to the packing shed), a very popular crabbing spot for families, and sticking to the furthest right channel, you'll slowly see the 'Strood' become visible. Be mindful to give yourself enough space away from the warning triangles, which mark out groynes at high tide. Once closer to the road, there are the famous creeks you can explore! This is a twisting maze of marshland, with some creeks that end abruptly and others that create a unique passageway towards the Strood.

The land by the road is jetski club grounds; however, they are usually happy enough to share. From here, if the tide is above 5m the road (B1025) will begin to flood. The higher the tide (biggest usually around 5.8m) the more water will cover the road. A true spectacle to experience. Be careful of moving traffic, as not everyone chooses to stop! If

ABOVE View of the Hammerhead Jetty.

LEFT Paddling past Packing Shed Island at sunrise.

planned correctly, you can paddle towards the road with the incoming tide, and back to your starting point with the outgoing tide. Note: this paddle doesn't work at low tide, as you'll run out of water towards the road, being left in the mud.

The total round-trip paddle is approximately 6km, and you can easily spend time at the Strood watching the road flood/exploring more of the creeks. If you can manage this with a sunrise, depending on conditions, you'll truly be rewarded with calm seas and pink skies!

Wildlife
There is always a chance to see a seal during this paddle; however, as the area has increased in popularity, sightings are becoming more rare. Even rarer would be a porpoise sighting, which is possible in the main channel! You will get to see plenty of wildlife, though, mostly gulls and oystercatchers. During the warmer months there are often swarms of jellyfish in the area.

Food stops
Right behind the car park in Mersea you'll find the Blackwater Pearl café. Just along from the café is the Coast Inn, and a little further along you'll find The Victory pub. All serve great food and drinks, and there's plenty of outdoor seating available.

Mersea is famous for its seafood, so be sure to try some of the local restaurants and kiosks selling fresh local produce!

Other activities
Boat trips of all kinds operate from here, from fishing trips to sightseeing trips, while you can even grab a cream tea at the Packing Shed (www.packing-shed.org.uk/).

East of England Paddlesports hosts lots of events in Mersea. Our most popular social paddle is this Strood paddle, where we paddle out to watch the road flood and explore the nearby creeks. We've had upwards of 80 people exploring the creeks and lining the road, watching it submerge as the tide comes in. We also run lots of night paddles in the area, including sunrise and sunset paddles. Find out more at: www.facebook.com/groups.eoeps.

ESSEX

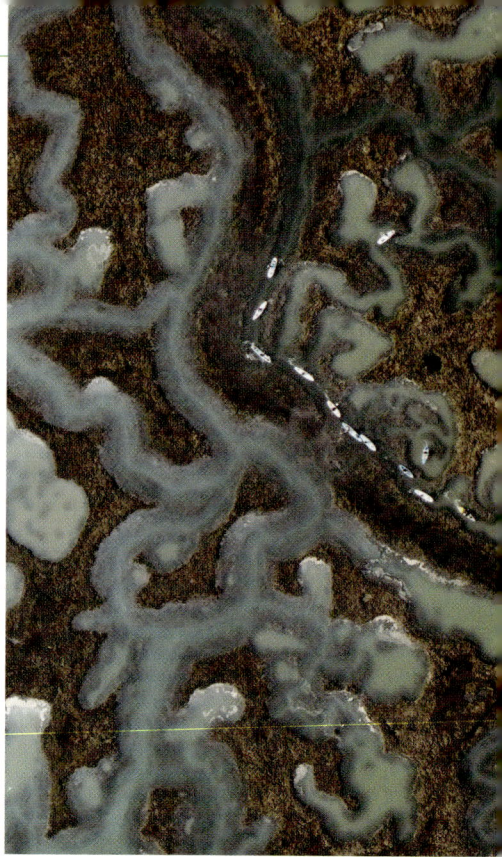

NEED TO KNOW

■ As this is a tidal section of the Colne Estuary, you don't need a licence to paddle, but timing is critical for launch (see page 12 for more information).

■ Check tide times and height of tide to ensure there's plenty of water to complete the paddle. Make sure you check the wind speed and direction, too.

■ You should aim to be at the Strood for high tide.

■ Always paddle within your capabilities.

■ Footwear is important due to the oyster shells dotted about the coastline in Mersea Island.

■ Do not obstruct traffic on the Strood causeway.

ABOVE Exploring the creek that runs alongside the road.

TOP RIGHT Line of paddlers exploring the creeks at high tide.

RIGHT Mersea's colourful beach huts.

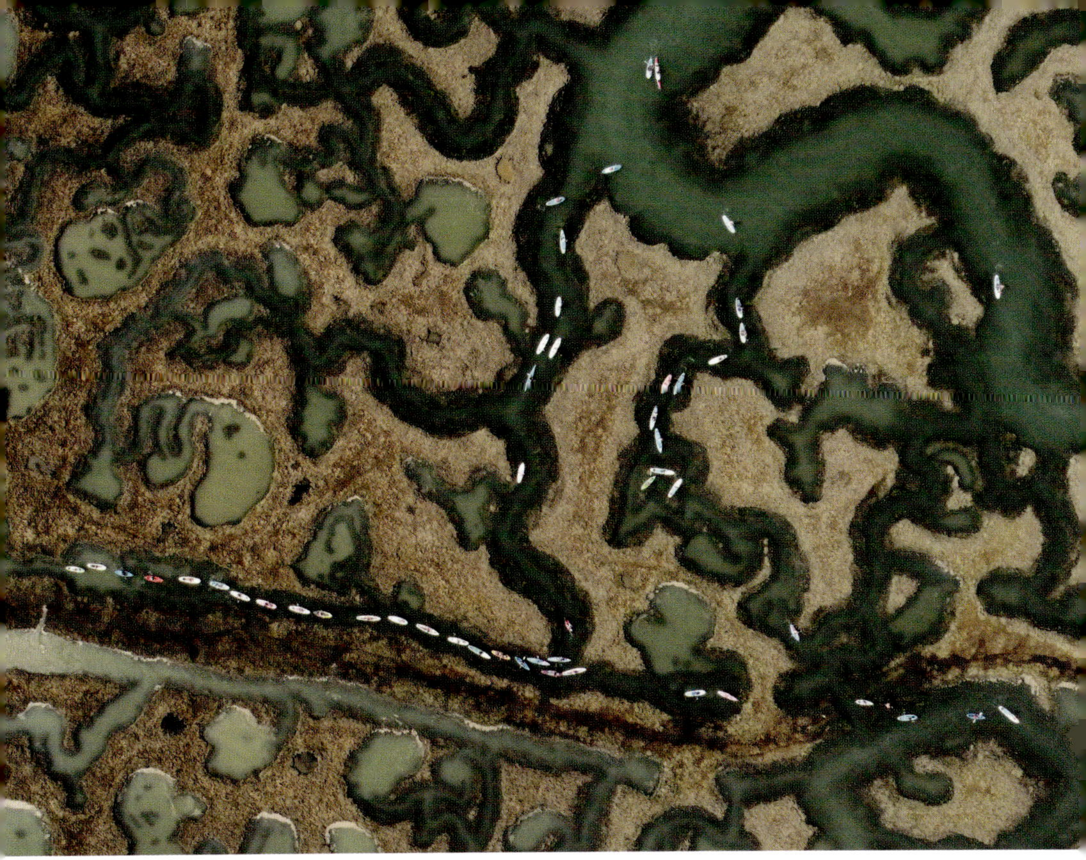

14 MERSEA ISLAND CIRCUMNAVIGATION

Mersea Island sits in the Blackwater and Colne estuaries to the south of Colchester. Lots of paddle routes are available from Mersea; however being tidal, you'll need to have an understanding of the tides before setting out. Saying that, being an estuary, this is a fairly safe area to paddle, with access to the water at high and low tide – so expect to see lots of kayakers, paddleboarders and rowers here. Footwear is advised at all times due to the nature of the ground: a mix of rocks, mud and sand – with lots of sharp oyster shells.

The Lowdown

DISTANCE 20km
WATER TYPE Tidal
DIFFICULTY ●●●
LICENCE REQUIRED ✗

PARKING **37 Victoria Esplanade** West Mersea, Colchester CO5 8BH, ///poodle.inert.march. Open March–October. Height barrier 2.2m. Pay and display at time of writing. Toilet facilities across the road. Approx. 150 spaces. **Seaview Avenue** West Mersea, Colchester CO5 8DA, ///home.comforted.dockers. Open year-round. Height barrier 2.5m. Pay and display at time of writing. Facilities a short walk away at Victoria Esplanade (above).

LAUNCH POINT **Victoria Esplanade** ///speedy.loopholes.senses. Head down between the famous colourful beach huts of Mersea on to the beach. **Seaview Avenue** ///data.juices.clouding. Short walk across the road, towards the beach.

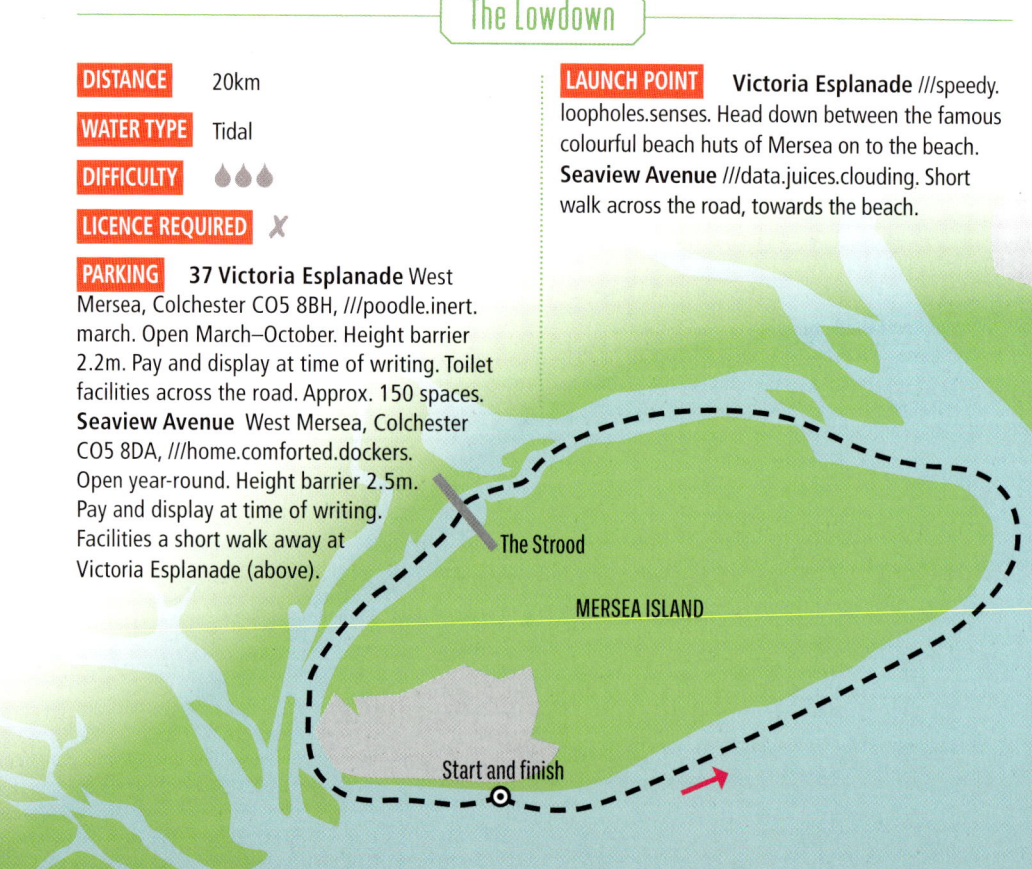

MERSEA ISLAND CIRCUMNAVIGATION

History

Mersea's name comes from the Old English word Meresig, meaning 'island of the pool'. Mersea Island is the most easterly inhabited island in Britain. The island is split into two main areas, West and East Mersea, and is connected to the mainland by the Strood, a causeway that can flood at high tide – making Mersea a true island. The harbour in West Mersea is used by fishing vessels year-round, producing lots of fresh produce, including world-famous oysters!

The paddle

This paddle requires a bit of planning. The ideal tide height is over 5m (check local tide times for Mersea Island) and obviously it's preferable to have low wind. This paddle is around 20km with very few spots to evacuate, especially around the east end of the island. Conditions will decide whether you launch from the beach and go left or right. The key is to be at the Strood for high tide, so you can float your craft across the road.

Our preferred route, then, would be to launch and turn left, heading towards East Mersea first. You'll see Bradwell Power Station in the distance. Going this way, you'll pass several caravan sites, one of which is Coopers Beach, and an outdoor centre (Essex Outdoors). You'll reach Mersea Stone, the corner that sits opposite Point Clear and Brightlingsea.

From here you'll start to be assisted by the incoming tide, and as you turn left around the corner the water can rush quite fast – a wide turn works best, heading in towards Pyefleet Channel/Creek. Plenty of activity happens around here, from foot ferries travelling between Mersea and

TOP Pausing on Mersea Stone Beach before paddling around into Pyefleet Creek.

BOTTOM Ready to launch from the Esplanade.

Brightlingsea, to several sailing clubs, school groups and fishing vessels. Hugging the land on the left, follow it until you see the Strood – the road that connects Mersea to the mainland. Just before the road, on your left, keep your eyes peeled for some random chairs! We're not entirely sure of the story behind these, though the most logical reason would be for birdwatching, as there are four poles we assume would be for attaching camouflage netting.

To cross the road takes a little patience, especially if vehicles are still passing. The easiest option is to get out on the right, and either float craft through the barriers or lift over. Please be responsible by the road. The opposite side has more space, and benches (the area is managed by the local jetski club; however, they are usually happy enough to share).

Often, on bigger tides the atmosphere here is fantastic, with a mix of boats, kayaks, SUPs, canoes, occasionally windsurfs, foils and waterskis, whose owners will all most likely pause to watch the road flood and sarcastically cheer on any road users trying to pass! This is also a good spot to pause for lunch. From here you are about two thirds of the way. You can head back with the outgoing tide. Be sure to give the groynes alongside the mainland on your left a bit of space (marked with warning triangles). When you get closer to the harbour, be mindful of boat moorings and moving traffic (fishing boats, day trip boats and swimmers) and people crabbing off the Jetty. You can pause here for a drink/snack. The Blackwater Pearl café is just behind the jetty and, if open, use the toilet facilities in the Coast Road car park.

You'll then carry on heading towards Packing Shed Island, which you should be able to see just ahead of you. You have options here. We would favour hugging the mainland, although the flow between Cobmarsh Island and Monkey Beach can be quite fast and messy. If this looks too much for you (white caps, faster flowing water, bigger swell etc), you could paddle

between Cobmarsh and Packing Shed and take a wide birth back towards the mainland. You'll then be paddling past some impressive looking properties and then the colourful beach huts!

On 4 August 2023, the East of England Paddlesports admin team took on a challenge to circumnavigate Mersea island on a Mega SUP (an eight-person paddleboard), which we managed to achieve in an impressive 4 hours and 42 minutes, raising over £2,000 for the Royal National Lifeboat Institution. Our adventure was featured in local papers and on local radio stations, and we even appeared in an article for *Stand Up Paddle Mag UK!*

Wildlife

There is always a chance to see a seal during this paddle; however, as the area has increased in popularity, sightings are becoming more rare. Even rarer would be a porpoise sighting, which is possible in the main channel! You will get to see plenty of wildlife, though, mostly gulls and oystercatchers. During the warmer months there are often swarms of jellyfish in the area.

Food stops

Right behind the car park in Mersea you'll find the Blackwater Pearl café. Just along from the café is the Coast Inn, and a little further along you'll find The Victory pub. All serve great food and drinks, and there's plenty of outdoor seating available.

Mersea is famous for its seafood, so be sure to try some of the local restaurants and kiosks selling fresh local produce!

Other activities

As this is quite a long paddle, you may choose to make a weekend of it. There are various campsites and caravan parks and lots a bars and restaurants to choose from. We like Coopers Beach, which is close to the launch point – airbnb.com/h/eoeps.

NEED TO KNOW

- Check tide times and height of tide to ensure there's plenty of water to complete the paddle. Make sure you check the wind speed and direction, too.
- You should aim to be at the Strood for high tide.
- Always paddle within your capabilities.
- Footwear is important due to the oyster shells dotted about the coastline in Mersea Island.
- Do not obstruct traffic on the Strood causeway.

ABOVE Ted having a paddle.
LEFT Random Chairs!
OVERLEAF Birdseye view of Mersea Island.

SUFFOLK

Suffolk, sitting in the heart of the East of England, is bordered by Norfolk, Essex and Cambridgeshire. The county has an area approximately 1,466 sq miles.

The Suffolk coastline spans for around 50 miles and is often formed of London clay and chalk, which means the coastline is very susceptible to erosion. Along the coastline you will find the River Deben, Orwell and Stour. (This book contains a lot of paddles across these rivers.)

Along the coastline you're likely to find sandy beaches in the south of the county and rugged cliff lines with shingle beaches to the north, following the powerful effects of the North Sea. The Suffolk Coast Path, which spans 50 miles, offers views of this coastline and give people the opportunity to take in the stunning scenery.

As well as the rugged coastline, there are many nature reserves which are ran by the RSPB, offering an opportunity to see a vast array of wildlife.

Whether you seek relaxation on a sandy beach or adventure on the dramatic cliffs, Suffolk's coastline has something to offer everyone.

TOP Scorched Tree.

RIGHT Orwell Bridge at sunset.

15 WALDRINGFIELD

Waldringfield is a small village town in the east of Suffolk, just 12.9km to the east of Ipswich. The river Deben is a tidal river running roughly 40km, passing lots of untouched countryside and farming land, and ending at the North Sea at Bawdsey. Waldringfield is an ideal spot for a paddle, with a few options. You can always access the water here no matter what state of the tide, though this will give limitations on how far you can paddle. With the river being tidal and fast-flowing, a good understanding of tide times and currents is important. The banks can be really muddy at lower tides, so footwear is advised. There is lots of boat activity year-round so be considerate of other water users. There are other spots along the river which make for nice paddles, though Waldringfield is one of our favourites.

WALDRINGFIELD

The Lowdown

DISTANCE 15km/10km

WATER TYPE Tidal/river

DIFFICULTY

LICENCE REQUIRED ✗

PARKING **Maybush Inn** Cliff Rd, Waldringfield, Woodbridge IP12 4QL, ///crusher.sideboard.beanbag. Pay and display at time of writing. Two areas: Maybush patrons (free up to 3 hr); visitors (£1 charge >3 hr or £5/day).

LAUNCH POINT From **Maybush Inn car park** (above): ///plump.populate.passion. Carry equipment down a narrow set of stairs in the far corner, opposite the end of the pub, or walk around the pub and down to the beach to avoid the steps. Be careful to avoid swimmers near the bottom of the steps. Launch straight onto the water from the beach.

At low tide, head to the right-hand side to find a more suitable area to launch, though it can still be quite muddy: ///argued.envoy.cute.

BELOW Roadside launch ramp.

History

Waldringfield is 6.4km from the historic market town of Woodbridge and roughly 12.9km from Ipswich. The village is surrounded by farmland and lies within the Suffolk Coasts and Heaths National Landscape. Nearby Woodbridge town lies at the head of the River Deben Estuary, about 16km from the North Sea. Originally a Saxon settlement, it is near the site of the Sutton Hoo ship burial, one of the most extraordinary archaeological finds in history (see Other activities, below). Ships for the Royal Navy were at one time built here.

The paddle

From the launch point you have two options: left towards Woodbridge/Wilford Bridge or right towards the Ramsholt Arms.

Wilford Bridge To Wilford Bridge, it's 15km there and back. Launch and turn left. Once you pass the small boatyard, head left and wind your way upstream. You'll pass Martlesham Creek on your left. Keep paddling straight, towards the village you can see dead ahead, and you'll then start to see Woodbridge train station, which can offer a good spot to pause, turn around or end your journey.

For a longer paddle, up to Wilford Bridge, keep paddling in the same direction and you'll pass Tidemill Yacht Harbour, some wetlands, old boat wrecks, some very cool-looking 'scorched' trees – at which point you should head towards the

left of the river to avoid paddling into the Saltings. You'll see some netting and fencing separating the river – at high tide you may be able to pass through this, though it would be best to stick to the left! Be aware that there are lots of underwater obstructions here running along the fence line.

Keep paddling and eventually you'll see Wilford Bridge ahead of you. If you can reach here as the tide turns, you'll enjoy an easier paddle downstream back to Waldringfield. If going this direction, remember this section of the River Deben is tidal and so you need to be on the water roughly two hours either side of high tide when you get towards Woodbridge, otherwise you'll run out of water and have to do the 'muddy walk of shame'!

Ramsholt Arms

To the Ramsholt Arms, it's roughly 10km there and back. Please note,

TOP Paddling past the entrance to Tide Mill Yacht Harbour.

ABOVE One of many old boat wrecks along the Deben.

RIGHT The Wilford Bridge on approach.

this is a tidal section, so plan all journeys around the tide times.

Launch from the same spot as above and head towards the right. You'll pass heathland and fields, so please be considerate when paddling among wildlife and other water users. Conditions with less wind would be favourable for this paddle, as it's quite an open stretch of water.

The Ramsholt Arms is a large traditional pub, with a big outdoor dining area, good for a summer social evening paddle. From here, simply reverse your paddle and head back to Waldringfield. Roughly halfway back is a small beach, known locally as 'The Rocks'. This is a nice area to stop and have a drink.

Wildlife
This area hosts a huge variety of birdlife, including various gull species, grey heron and little egret. Paddlers can also be treated to a seal when conditions are good, quite often close by.

Food stops
Parking is at the Maybush Inn, a very nice traditional pub ran by Deben Inns. If you stop at Woodbridge, there are lots of options in the village, including the usual shops and cafés – the Two Magpies Bakery and café serves delicious cakes, pastries and breads.

Many pubs in Woodbridge serve local ales and there is also an Adnams shop selling beer, wine and handcrafted spirits near the railway station in town.

Other activities
The Suffolk Coast & Heaths National Landscape offers plenty of walking and cycling options for you to make the most of this stunning region.

For all those interested in history, the Sutton Hoo royal burial site, managed by the National Trust, is a must-see. One of the most extraordinary archaeological discoveries of all time – a 27m long Anglo-Saxon ship housing a burial chamber fit for a king – was uncovered in 1939. Visit the National Trust website for more information: www.nationaltrust.org.uk/visit/suffolk/sutton-ho/.

If you have time for a longer trip, you could catch the Felixstowe Foot and Bicycle Ferry from Old Felixstowe to Harwich (https://www.harwichharbourferry.com/timetables). From Harwich it is possible to

LEFT Paddling back through the Wilford Bridge.
BELOW Ramsholt Arms Pub.

get a ferry to the Netherlands! Though if you fancy a shorter, more local ferry trip during the summer months, you can go from Bawdsey Quay to Old Felixstowe and back (https://www.boathousescafebawdsey.co.uk/out-and-about). Wave the bat at the end of the jetty to call the ferryman. There are also lots of wild swimming groups that meet along the coast year-round.

NEED TO KNOW

■ This is a tidal river, so you don't need a licence to paddle, but please check tide times and launch accordingly (see page 12 for more information). Ensure you check the wind speed and direction, too, especially if you plan to head towards the Ramsholt Arms.

■ Always paddle within your capabilities.

■ This can be a busy area, so please respect navigation rules, and keep right and clear of channels where possible.

16 SUDBURY TO THE HENNY SWAN

Sudbury is an old market town situated on the River Stour in the south-west of Suffolk, and set within a National Landscape. The historic markets date back as far as the early 11th century. Even today, the market still happens twice a week.

ABOVE Calm River Stour.

SUDBURY TO THE HENNY SWAN

The Lowdown

DISTANCE 7km
WATER TYPE River
DIFFICULTY
LICENCE REQUIRED
(see Need to know box)

PARKING **The Granary** Quay Ln, Sudbury CO10 2AN, ///intestine.stared.loaf.

LAUNCH POINT Public pontoon ///messy.commander.supporter. At top of Granary car park (above), between two buildings.

History
Similar to its neighbouring town Dedham, Sudbury is well known for its artistic history, as it is here, in 1727, the great Thomas Gainsborough was born. Gainsborough was the leading portrait painter in the 18th century and a founding member of the Royal Academy. Gainsborough's House opened to the public as a museum in 1961 and has a large collection of his oil paintings and other artifacts on display.

The paddle
After parking up, head towards the public pontoon at the top of the car park, between the two buildings. Once on the water, continue straight, passing Sudbury Rowing Club on your right, until you reach the main stretch of the river. Turn left and travel with the flow of the river.

Now you are on the main river. After high periods of rainfall you may find that the river is flowing quickly, so take extra caution. Continue paddling past Friars Meadow on your left, which is a great spot for a picnic or to sit a while and enjoy the scenery. After a short distance you'll reach the weir. Keep left, where you'll see the one and only portage point on the right-hand side. Follow the steps down to the bottom of the weir, where you'll find the pontoon

BELOW Sudbury to Henry Swan.

to continue your journey. You'll now be at one with nature, with very little around you aside from trees, shrubs and fields. Be sure to look out for wildlife along this lovely stretch of the river.

Continue following the river, which bends round to the left and then again shortly to the right. You'll now reach the Henny Swan pub. Take extra caution and keep to the right as you approach, due to the small weir opposite the pontoon.

Once you've had a rest, turn around and retrace your route, taking in the sights that are not visible from the other direction.

Wildlife

The River Stour is a haven for all sorts of wildlife, and on this paddle you can expect to see owls, bats, kingfishers, swans, ducks, butterflies, damselflies and fish. You may even be lucky enough to spot an otter.

Food stops

With the launch point being near the town, you'll find many shops, cafés and pubs for something to eat. However, the Henny Swan comes highly recommended and has a comprehensive menu: www.thehennyswan.co.uk/.

Other activities

As the launch spot is so close to the main town, and with the amount of history in the town, there are plenty of activities off the water. You could visit Gainsborough's House to learn more about his life and marvel at his artistry: https://gainsborough.org/. Or, head to the Sudbury Quay Theatre to catch a show: https://quaysudbury.com/.

If you'd prefer to spend more time in nature, simply head for a walk along the river and down the old disused railway line, known as the Sudbury Railway Walk.

NEED TO KNOW

- As with most inland rivers and waterways, you need a licence from either Paddle UK or the Environment Agency to paddle the River Stour (see page 12 for more information).

- This river is a popular rowing spot and often hosts races, so ensure you give way to them.

BELOW East of England Paddlesports social paddle.

17 PIN MILL TO ORWELL BRIDGE

The River Orwell flows from Ipswich to Shotley in Suffolk, widening, from a river to an estuary. Above Stoke Bridge in Ipswich the river is known as the River Gipping, and at Shotley it joins the River Stour. The Orwell and Stour then join to form the Harwich Harbour, before flowing into the North Sea. At this point, it is also host to the UK's largest container port at Felixstowe.

The Lowdown

DISTANCE 3–15km

WATER TYPE Tidal river

DIFFICULTY

LICENCE REQUIRED ✗

PARKING For this section of the River Orwell parking is a small pay and display car park at Pin Mill, Chelmondiston IP9 1JJ, ///relishes.deaf.stated.

LAUNCH POINT Public slipway next to the Butt & Oyster pub, Pinmill Rd, Chelmondiston IP9 1JW, ///clipped.boast.circus. A short walk down the hill from the car park at Pin Mill (above).

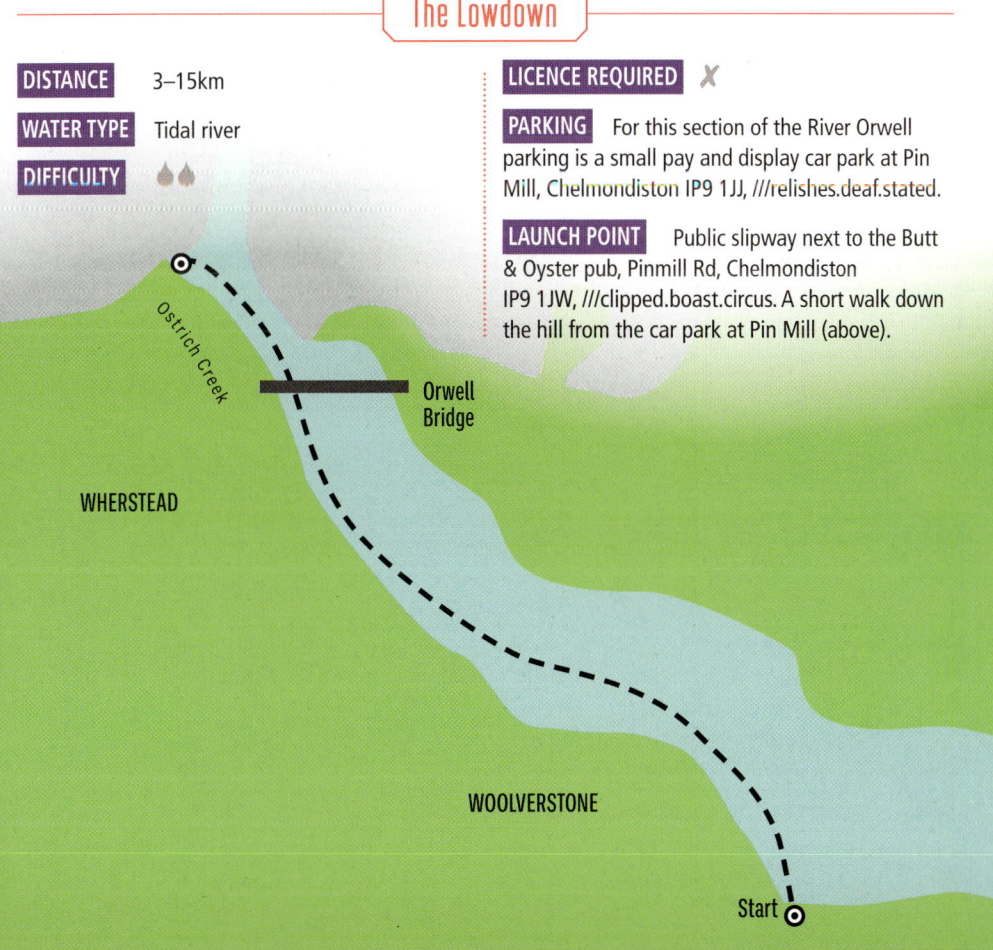

PADDLE THE EAST OF ENGLAND

The Orwell Bridge carries the A14 trunk road over the estuary to the south of Ipswich and it is this bridge our paddle is centred on, as it takes us from Pin Mill to the Ipswich city centre.

History

The Orwell has been a major shipping area for centuries, the Ipswich Dock having been in operation since the 7th century. In 1842, the newly opened wet dock was the largest in the UK at the time. Today it hosts a large marina which, via a sea lock, is home to many sailors and boatbuilders. The author and journalist Eric Blair loved the area so much that he made it his pen name: George Orwell.

Pin Mill, the south bank of the River Orwell and where this paddle starts, was once a busy cargo landing area, and many Thames sailing barges have been repaired here over the decades. The hamlet, including the Butt & Oyster pub that sits alongside this paddle's launch, reportedly played key roles in the smuggling industry. It also played a vital role in the Second World War, as it was home to the Royal Navy motor launches and tank landing craft used in the Normandy landings. These days it is a much quieter area, but appears in many books, TV programmes and films due to the stunning scenery.

The Orwell Bridge was opened in 1982 and carries the A14 over the river. At the time the central 190m-long span was the longest pre-stressed concrete span in use in the UK. It is in fact two bridges side by side (only visible from below the bridge), and is over 40m above you in the middle.

The paddle

Setting off from the launch point, paddle to the left with the incoming tide along the western shoreline, past

RIGHT Paddlers ready to launch at Pin Mill.

several houseboats and the Pin Mill Sailing Club. After passing some farmland you will shortly glimpse Woolverstone Hall, a Grade I listed building built in 1776 and widely thought to be one of the finest examples of Palladian architecture in England. It has had various uses over the centuries, but since 1992 has been the home of Ipswich High School and a country house wedding venue.

Next along the river is the Royal Harwich Yacht Club (RHYC), the royal patronage of which dates back to Queen Adelaide in 1845. At one point, Queen Victoria was an honorary member. With a rich sailing history, the club has seen action as far afield as Antarctica and competed in the prestigious America's Cup sailing competition. Next to RHYC is Woolverstone Marina, which is also the location of sailing school, and a campsite with woodland lodges.

Continuing along the shoreline past a large private house on the riverbank, the next view among the trees and parkland is Freston Tower, a six-storey folly built around 1578 by the wealthy landowner and trader Thomas Gooding. After a long and varied history, it was eventually gifted to the Landmark Trust in 1999 and is now available to rent as a holiday home, providing epic views from its 26 windows.

The land now flattens out toward the Orwell Bridge. The road that runs alongside the river here is called The Strand and can flood a little on very high tides. It is possible to park in some laybys here and launch, but only an hour or so either side of high tide, and care must be taken as it is very muddy in the shallows here.

You are now at the Orwell Bridge with its seven legs sat on concrete piers in the river. The widest span is used as the main shipping lane, so beware of river traffic. As you paddle under the bridge you can look up and see the gap between the two carriageways, which isn't visible from the road itself.

From here you enter into the more commercial and industrial area of the river.

On the left is Fox's Marina and the Orwell Yacht Club via Ostrich Creek, which can be paddled into, although beware that at high tide there's not enough clearance to paddle past the old road bridge and into Belstead Brook.

On the right now is the main port area where most of the large ships are docked and loaded.

Further along, the river splits into two. On the right is the main sea lock into Ipswich Marina, which is not accessible to paddlers. On the left, the tidal river continues into and through Ipswich, where it becomes the River Gipping. It is possible to paddle along here until the tide turns and begins to flood back out. Once the tide starts to turn, turn around and simply return the way you came.

Wildlife

The river, with its mudflats, salt marshes and parkland, is a haven for all sorts of wildlife. You will likely see herons and egrets fishing along the bank, while flocks of oystercatchers and redshanks make this their home. Seals are regularly spotted along the river, sometimes sunbathing near the bridge.

Food stops

There are limited landing points on this paddle so a picnic on the water is more likely, but within an hour or so of high tide you could pause on the very small beach at Stoke Sailing Club.

The obvious choice for food is the Butt & Oyster pub, which is right next to the launch point and is a traditional pub serving food and real ale: www.debeninns.co.uk/buttandoyster/.

Another good option after your paddle would be to visit the Suffolk Food Hall, which directly overlooks the bridge and has restaurants and cafés serving breakfast, lunch and afternoon tea: https://suffolkfoodhall.co.uk/.

Other activities

Pin Mill sits along the Suffolk Coastal Path, which is signposted. This section, known as the Stour and Orwell Walk (64km), connects the Sandlings Walk, the Essex Way and the Stour Valley Path: www.discoversuffolk.org.uk/stour-and-orwell-walk/.

The River Orwell is also home to many sailing clubs, ranging from small touring and racing clubs to larger yacht clubs and marinas.

You can even take advantage of a local tour company and see the bridge from the river without the effort of paddling on the Lady Orwell via a Thames river cruiser, built in 1979 and brought to Ipswich for sightseeing trips.

ABOVE Canoe resting with the view of the Orwell Bridge.

BELOW LEFT A rainbow of kayaks launching at Pin Mill.

NEED TO KNOW

- As this is a tidal river leading to an estuary there is no need for a licence (see page 12 for more information).
- Care should be taken, as large ships do still pass up and down the river. The central channel is clearly marked with large red and green buoys.
- Launch two to three hours either side of high tide to avoid getting stranded in the mud at the end of the public slipway.
- Launching with the incoming tide aiming to be under the bridge and toward Ipswich at high tide allows you to return with the outgoing tide. Depending on the wind conditions, it can sometimes get a little choppy.

18 BURES TO LAMARSH

Bures is a pretty village split in two by the River Stour, which forms the boundary between the Essex parish known as Bures Hamlet and the Suffolk parish known as Bures St Mary. The Stour is best known for running from Sudbury to Cattawade, with Bures being almost a third of the way downstream from the market town of Sudbury.

ABOVE A kayaker just upstream of Lamarsh Weir.

The Lowdown

DISTANCE 7–15km

WATER TYPE River

DIFFICULTY ◆

LICENCE REQUIRED ✓
(see Need to know box)

PARKING **Bures Community Centre**
Nayland Road, Bures CO8 5BX,
///bedrooms.wipe.hairspray. Parking is free, with 40 available spaces, and is located at the northern edge of the village.

LAUNCH POINT **Millennium Footbridge**
///foods.freshest.squirted. From the car park on Nayland Road (above) it's a flat 400–500m walk across the playing fields, past the cricket club, to the launch point next to the bridge.

History

Nestled in the Stour Valley, the village of Bures is home to many 16th-century buildings, but also the ancient St Stephens Chapel, which is reported to stand on the site where Edmund was crowned on Christmas Day 855 as the King of East Anglia, only to be killed some 10 years later by the Vikings as they invaded the region.

In more modern times the village celebrated the Millennium with the installation of a new footbridge over the River Stour, next to where this paddle begins.

The paddle

If you have walked from the Community Centre and not crossed the river, then from this side of the River Stour the paddle heads to the right, or upstream against the flow. Once launched, the paddle takes you through the village and under the old road bridge carrying the B1508. You are now heading out of the village, past some lovely houses with pontoons directly onto the river. The Stour continues north alongside the B1508 for a while and then a sharp left-hand bend in the river gets you heading west into the beautiful scenery of the Stour Valley.

As you paddle between the reeds and bulrushes you turn again to head north, and here you may spot a train on the Sudbury to Marks Tey branch line, which also stops at Bures, making it possible to travel here by train. Bures station is a 10–12-minute walk to the launch point and is mainly flat.

You will know if you are getting close to the first weir at Lamarsh as the river narrows, becoming a little more twisty, and you'll usually hear the weir before you see it. There are some lovely willow trees on your left, which have been grazed by the local cows and now follow the shape of the land.

The weir is just over 3km from the launch point and is a simple concrete weir with a central chute. The portage to continue is to the right-hand side with a set of wooden steps, which take you up above the weir for a lovely view of the Stour Valley.

On past Lamarsh, the river opens out a little and is covered with lily pads in the summer. A further 3km or so along sees you arrive towards Pitmire Weir (also known as Daws Weir). The approach can be quite overgrown in the summer and there are two routes, one directly ahead, and one which spurs off to the right in a short semicircle. Pitmire Weir is much higher than Lamarsh and very different in style, almost like a waterfall. The portage is to the right and again there's a few steps and a short walk to relaunch if you want to continue.

The next weir is around 2km further, past much more open meadows. This one, known as Shalford Weir, is a simple concrete lip across the river. Again, the portage is to your right and this is a perfect spot for a picnic on a sunny day with an open meadow to relax in.

At this point you are close to Great Henny, which is covered in another paddle in this

book from the village of Sudbury (see page 90).

The return paddle is downstream with options for more experienced paddlers in kayaks or canoes to shoot the weirs, particularly Lamarsh through its central channel. Obviously care should be taken and helmets are advised. Paddleboards are not suitable due to the fins, particularly at Pitmire due to its height.

Wildlife

There is lots of wildlife to see along this part of the Stour. Birdlife includes kingfishers, swans, herons, red kites and barn owls, to name a few, while the river is full of fish, from rudd and perch to pike. The section toward Lamarsh is farmland, so you may see dairy cows along the river and, if you're lucky, you may even spot deer. There are also reports of otter sightings, albeit rare.

Food stops

Lamarsh and Pitmire are remote rural locations so best suited to picnics. At the launch point in Bures, there are several brick BBQs for public use.

There are two pubs in Bures (The Eight Bells and The Three Horseshoes), both of which serve good food and have outside seating. There are also several cafés. If you choose to continue past Shalford Weir a short distance you'll also come to The Henny Swan pub: www.thehennyswan.co.uk/.

Other activities

It's worth seeking out the Bures Dragon hillside outline. Legend has it that in the early 1400s a fearsome dragon terrorised the local area and its skin was hard as metal or stone, repelling all arrows fired at it. In 2012, the dragon was immortalised in the landscape as part of Queen Elizabeth II's Diamond Jubilee celebrations, constructed from a 30cm-wide line of chalk. The dragon is on private land, but you can view it from the local bridlepaths or next to St Stephen's Chapel.

NEED TO KNOW

■ As with most inland rivers and waterways, you need a licence from either Paddle UK or the Environment Agency to paddle the River Stour (see page 12 for more information).

■ The section of the Stour is well known for its nesting swans, who are very protective of the area, so please take care.

■ From the launch there is an option to paddle downstream. However, the Bures Weir is not the easiest portage, and it may be best to launch further downstream and paddle back (maybe from Nayland).

■ The flow in this section of the river is normally quite light, particularly in the summer months with less rainfall.

LEFT The amazing Willow tree near Lamarsh Weir.
RIGHT The Bures Dragon from the air.

19 NAYLAND TO WISSINGTON WEIR

Nayland is situated 9.7km north of Colchester and 14.5km south of Sudbury, and sits at the heart of Dedham Vale, on the Suffolk side of the Essex and Suffolk border. The Anglo-Saxon name for Nayland was Eiland, meaning 'island', and the village was built on the higher ground in the river flood plain, to protect it from floods.

The Lowdown

DISTANCE 4.5km

WATER TYPE River

DIFFICULTY 💧

LICENCE REQUIRED ✓ (see Need to know box)

PARKING Bear Street Nayland CO6 4LR, ///thousands.custodian.hurls. Free at time of writing.

LAUNCH POINT Caley Green ///dusted.resources.nibbled

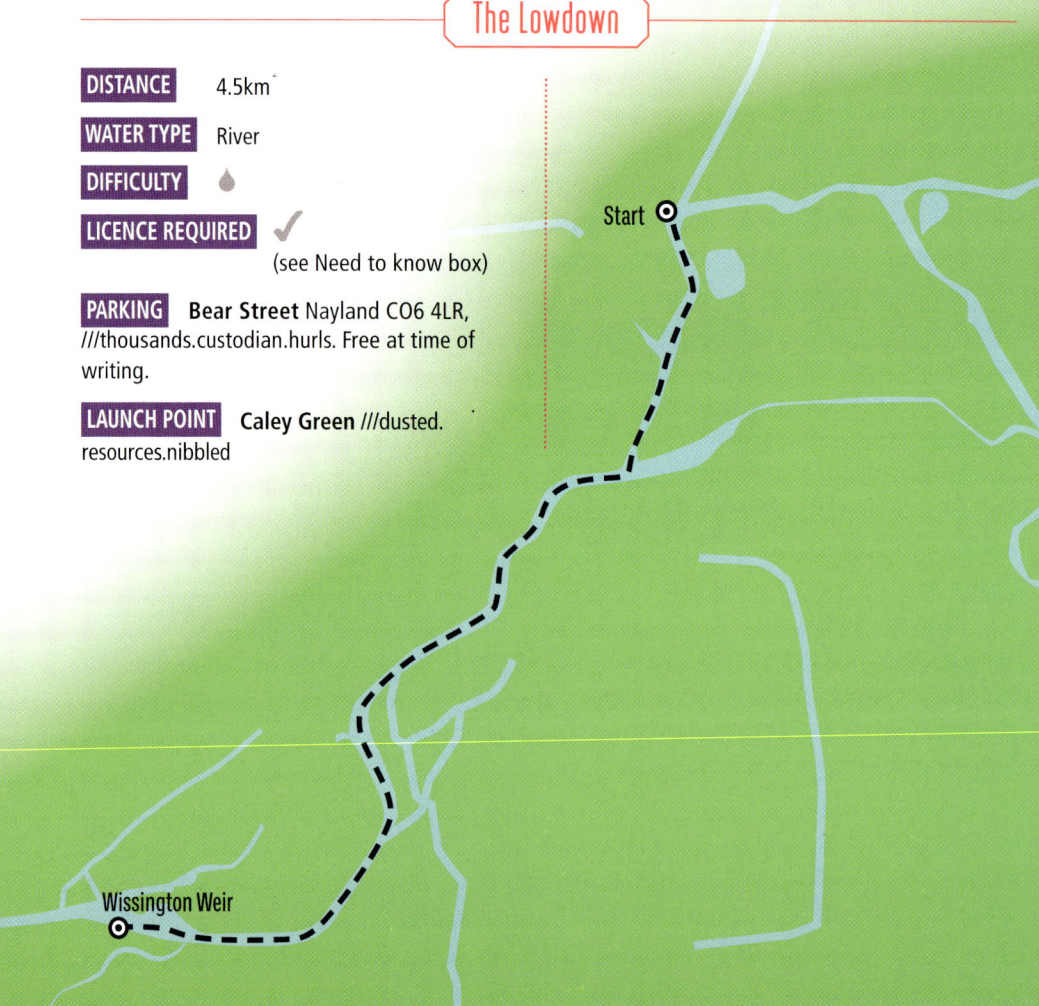

History

Nayland and the village at the end of this paddle, Wiston, were merged into one civil parish in 1884. As Nayland was built on higher ground, it provided a place for safe crossing of the flood plains, and became a prime location for trade, known for its cloth, soap and leather manufacturing. By the late Middle Ages it was holding a successful weekly market, and many rich merchants traded from here. As such, there are over 100 listed buildings in the village, dating back to the 14th century.

The paddle

Starting at Nayland (Bear Street), launch from Caley Green. This launch point is often shallow, so you may need to get into the water to get going! Once on the water, head right, upstream. The first stretch of this paddle is a windy stretch and is often overgrown, causing it to be narrow, resulting in river users having to clear their own path through, but it will open up. (Please note: any trees that are blocking the river should be reported to the Environment Agency). You will now reach a short tunnel, which goes under the main road from Colchester to Sudbury (A134). Following high periods of rain, the tunnel will have a strong flow, so take extra care. If you're on a SUP, mind your head in the tunnel as it varies in height.

ABOVE Misty day at Nayland.

Once out of the tunnel you will continue upstream until you meet the main stretch of the River Stour. At the junction, you'll need to turn right. Left will take you to a weir, where there is no through access.

Now you are on the main stretch of the river, and you'll soon see a small inlet of water on the right-hand side, which flows from the old mill. Continue on the main stretch of the river where you will pass under a footbridge. Here you will be able to see some of the remains of the old bridges still in the water. Follow until you reach Wissington Weir. As there are private fields on either side, and no direct access, the paddle is often stunning and quiet, so make sure you take in the peaceful sounds of nature.

As you approach Wissington Weir, on the right-hand side you will see Wiston Mill which was an old corn mill in 1674. The mill pond is a great place to stop and take in the surroundings, with the rushing waters of the weir flowing in the background.

Once at the weir, you've reached your turning point. If you want to continue on further, there is a portage on the left-hand side of the weir, which will take you up towards Sudbury.

Wildlife
On this paddle you could be treated to all sorts of wildlife, whether that be pike, grass snakes, otters, bats, and lots of birds including cormorants, red kites, herons and kingfishers.

Food stops
There are no food stops on this paddle; however, the Anchor Inn (Nayland), and The Angel and The Crown (Stoke by Nayland) are all a short car distance away.

Other activities
There are plenty of walks nearby from Nayland to other nearby villages.

NEED TO KNOW
- As with most inland rivers and waterways, you need a licence from either Paddle UK or the Environment Agency to paddle the River Stour (see page 12 for more information).
- The first part of this paddle is narrow and sometimes overgrown.
- Be mindful of the tunnel's variation in height, especially if you're on an SUP.

RIGHT Under the tunnel.

BELOW In the mill pond.

OVERLEAF The stunning three-level weir at Wissington.

20 STRATFORD ST MARY TO THE LANGHAM FLUMES

The charming village of Stratford St Mary is nestled in the heart of Suffolk's Constable Country. The renowned landscape painter was inspired by Stratford's beauty and captured it in several of his finest works. The village, together with the neighbouring hamlet of Higham, sits on the Essex and Suffolk border, right by the River Stour. This is a lesser-used section of the Stour, so on busier days this could be a good option, although parking is limited along the road.

The Lowdown

DISTANCE 7km

WATER TYPE River

DIFFICULTY 💧💧

LICENCE REQUIRED ✓ (see Need to know box)

PARKING **Lower Street** Stratford St Mary, CO7 6JR, ///shook.noses.muddy. Free at time of writing. Park right across from the launch point. Please be mindful of noise, as this is a residential area.

LAUNCH POINT ///enable.burglars.compelled. Walk down a footpath towards the weir, where you'll find a passageway and bridge across the river, towards the launch points. Head to the right and you'll see a wooden portage point: be sure to get on the correct side, otherwise you'll be paddling downstream towards Dedham. You want to be going upstream, against the flow, to get to the Langham Flumes.

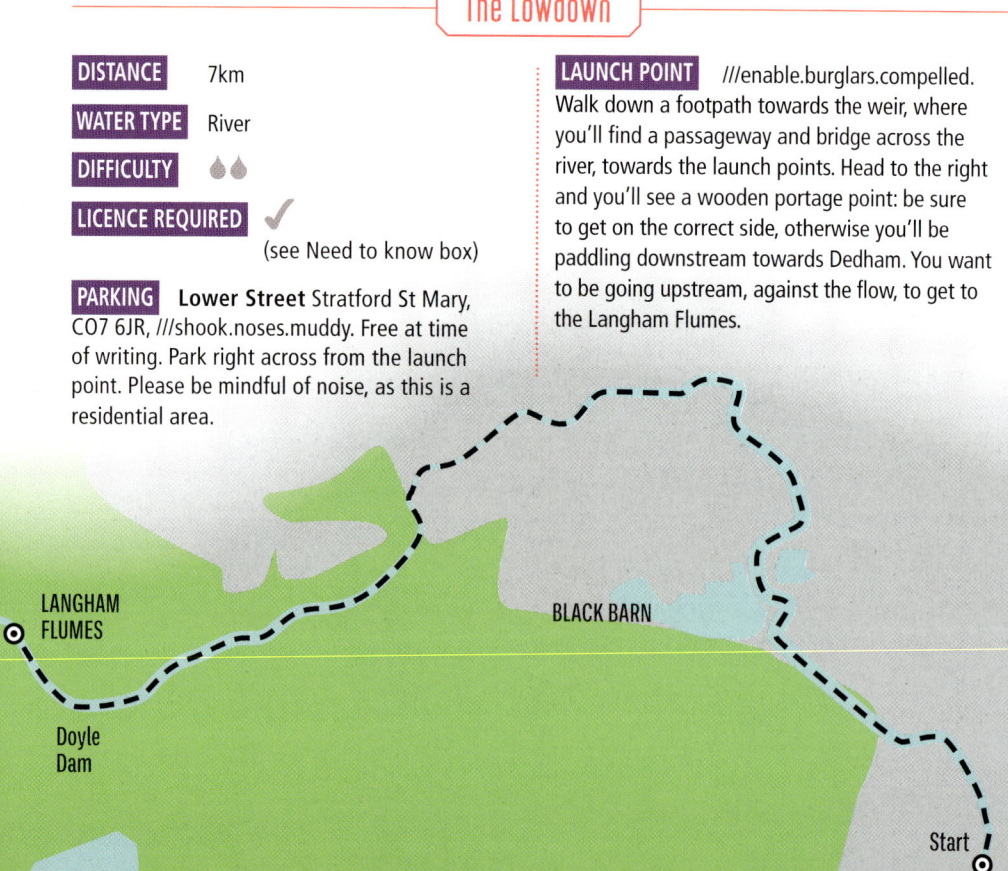

STRATFORD ST MARY TO THE LANGHAM FLUMES

History
Stratford St Mary has been around for a very long time! People have been living here as far back as 4,000 years ago. It was a Saxon settlement and later became rich through the wool trade. The village had a working mill on the River Stour for many years.

The Langham Flumes were originally built to divert water for a mill. Today, they are enjoyed by canoers and kayakers as a navigational stretch of moving water. Please be aware that the water levels can vary depending on the rainfall, and it's always a good idea to check the conditions before you go and wear suitable safety equipment.

The paddle
You'll be heading upstream, along a narrow part of the river. As this is a much more secluded part of the River Stour, be careful to avoid low-hanging trees and branches. Tress have occasionally fallen, too: be sure to report any fallen trees to the Environment Agency.

Launch from the portage, and make sure to head right. As you paddle, you'll come to a large corner, where you'll see some beautiful-looking properties to your right and a lovely weeping willow tree. As you paddle, the river constantly meanders and you'll find that you are soon surrounded by

PREVIOUS PAGE View from the launch.
LEFT Weeping willow tree.
BELOW Langham pumping station.

nature and away from the hustle and bustle of busy roads and towns. There may be the odd house or farm on this stretch, but be sure to take in the quiet atmosphere; this is a wonderful place to embrace all that nature provides, as there are frequently kingfishers, herons, swans and fish to be spotted on this stretch.

Eventually, you'll get up towards a bridge. This is the Langham pumping station. Built in the 1930s, it now uses electricity to lift river water for cleaning at a nearby water treatment plant. It's important because it keeps the local area supplied with fresh water, and it works with another station in Tiptree to prevent water shortages. It is a modern-looking white concrete building with a slanted roof.

As you continue on, you may start to notice that the flow becomes a bit stronger – this is because you're getting closer to the flumes. You will get to Doyle Dam first, a humanmade 'chute', which was built in 2007. This adds a little excitement to any navigation. On the left you'll see the portage point for the flumes. Be careful here, as the flow is much more noticeable. If you wish to carry on upstream, there's a short walk uphill to get past the flumes, where you'll see a portage point to launch. You can continue here towards Nayland – a really secluded stretch – and then on towards Wissington Weir (see our Nayland paddle for more information on this stretch, page 102).

Langham is a great place to stop and have a rest or picnic. Alternatively, if you're an experience paddler, you could paddle down the flumes. Please note, we advise against doing this on a SUP, due to the fins. This is a huge concrete structure, with rocks and fast-flowing water, originally built to divert water to help operate a mill, so please be sure to paddle within your capabilities and wear a helmet. Swimming is not permitted in this area.

When you're ready to head back, the return journey will be a breeze with the flow. With any moving water, you'll need to react quicker to the obstacles, corners, fallen trees and so on that come at you a lot faster!

For a shorter paddle to the Langham Flumes, there are often a few spaces around the road nearby to where the Flumes are, which would require a short walk to the river. Please check local signage for any parking restrictions.

Wildlife

As this stretch is secluded and away from busy roads and towns, it is a beautiful place to immerse yourself in nature. You're likely to see kingfishers darting around along with various other wildlife, such as herons, swans, red kites and cormorants. You might even spot the odd grass snake or otter! There are also some big fish on this stretch, so keep an eye out in the waters that surround you.

Food stops

There isn't really anywhere to stop for food along this stretch, so we advise packing snacks and/or a picnic. After the paddle, The Swan Inn on Lower Street, which offers fantastic food and drinks, makes for a nice return treat: www.stratfordswan.com/.

Other activities

As this is a rural area, it is light on other activities. However, down the road from Stratford St Mary, towards Dedham, is Hall Farm, which has a lovely café, farm shop and a farm trail. There are farm animals, picnic areas and various activities for children along the trail: https://hallfarmshop.com/.

RIGHT View of the Langham Flumes.
OVERLEAF Paddling up to Doyle Dam.

NEED TO KNOW

■ A Waterways Licence is required for this stretch of water (see page 12 for more information). Paddle UK offers good value membership, which includes access to the water, third party public liability insurance and various discounts nationwide.

■ Caution is required: this is a faster-flowing section of the Stour, and it's often overgrown, with the occasional underwater obstruction or branch that may catch the fin of a paddleboard.

■ There are no facilities in the immediate vicinity and parking is limited.

■ This is a residential area, so please be mindful when using electric pumps and avoid making loud noises.

NORFOLK

Norfolk is known as Nelsons County due to him being born here in 1758 and learning to sail here. A rich history of settlement exists here for over 1 million years including the Romans, Picts, and the home of Boudicca, Queen of the Iceni. Much of Norfolk history is closely entwined with that of Britain with revolution, crowning and deaths of early Kings and at one time it was the most densely populated area of the British Isle. It still boasts the highest concentration of churches in an area anywhere across the world.

Its links to Royalty continue to this day with the Royal Estate of Sandringham being a popular tourist attraction throughout the year.

Due to the flat nature of the county, many people refer to the area as the Country of the Endless Skies which is certainly true.

With over 80 miles of coastline, the area is unique in that you can watch the sunrise over the water at Great Yarmouth and sunset over the water at Hunstanton. In between, you'll find scenery featuring cliffs, sandy and stony beaches, and tidal estuaries to explore. Much of this is able to be paddled depending on conditions; even a little surfing is possible on the more northern section of the Coast.

With a varied landscape of Forests around Thetford in the south, the Fens (former marshland) to the west of the county, and the beautiful waterways of Norfolk Broads to the east, there really is something for everyone here.

The Broads National Park is a mecca for paddling enthusiasts. The Broads consist of a series of lakes and flooded peat workings covering an area of over 300 square kilometres with 7 rivers and 63 broads, most of which are able to be explored by kayak, SUP or canoe. More information about the Broads can be found here:

https://www.broads-authority.gov.uk/

TOP EOEPS paddle on the broads.

RIGHT A windmill on the Norfolk Broads.

21 COLTISHALL TO BUXTON MILL

Coltishall lies at the highest navigation point on the River Bure, north-east of Norfolk's main city and county town, Norwich. It's a popular village, especially in the height of summer, due to the ease of access to the river (the village is sometimes referred to as 'the Gateway to the Broads'). So, you'll find lots of other watercraft on the river, including canoes, kayaks and SUPs, and leisure boats.

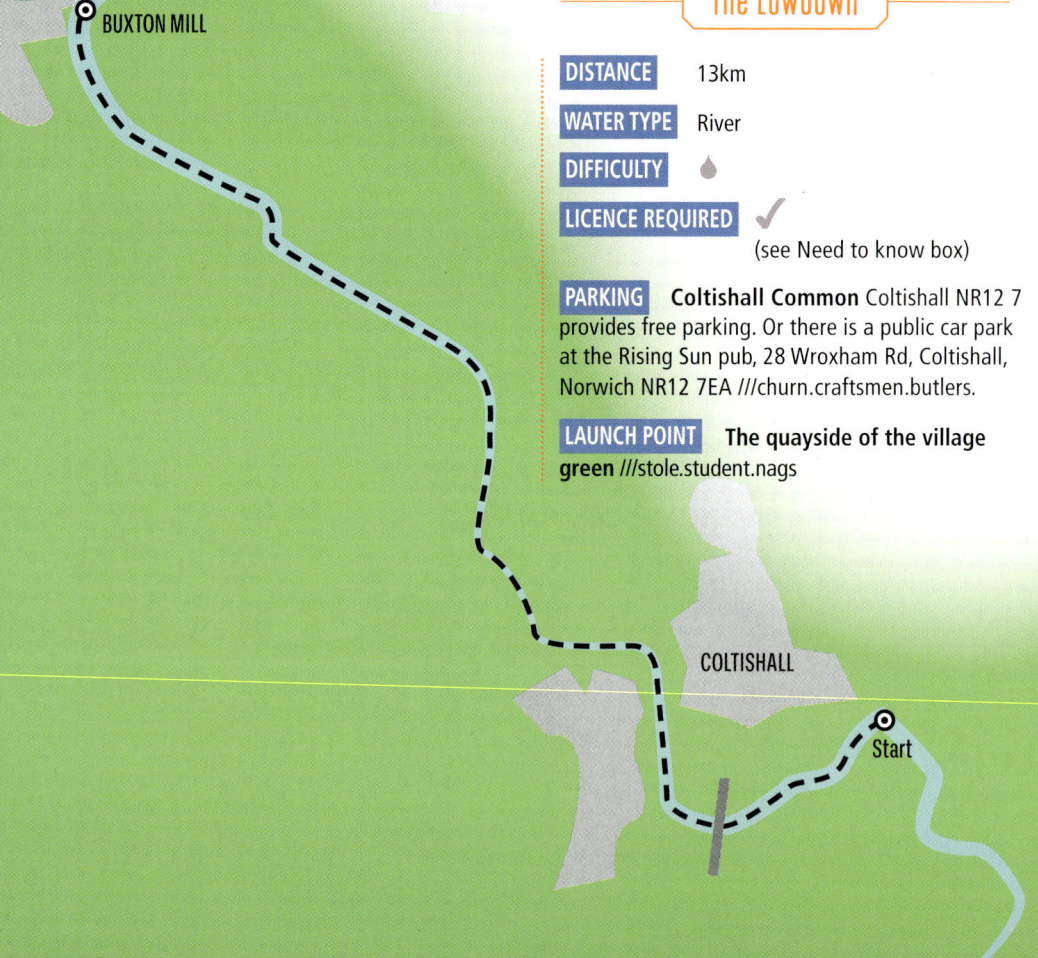

The Lowdown

DISTANCE 13km

WATER TYPE River

DIFFICULTY 💧

LICENCE REQUIRED ✓ (see Need to know box)

PARKING **Coltishall Common** Coltishall NR12 7 provides free parking. Or there is a public car park at the Rising Sun pub, 28 Wroxham Rd, Coltishall, Norwich NR12 7EA ///churn.craftsmen.butlers.

LAUNCH POINT **The quayside of the village green** ///stole.student.nags

History

As it is situated on the River Bure, Coltishall has always been an important route for trade between Aylsham and Great Yarmouth. In the late 18th and early 19th centuries, the village was home to a number of maltings and wholesale breweries, supplying well-known brands that are still popular today.

Coltishall is also famed for its boatbuilding industry, and especially Norfolk wherries, a craft specially designed for the narrow rivers in the area, such as the Bure. The wherries allowed for the fast transit of freight from the village to nearby ports, and the last-known trading wherry was launched in 1912.

RAF Coltishall, the home of the Hawker Hurricanes of the 242 squadron, opened in 1939. It was a fighter airfield during the Second World War, but it was shut down in 2006. It now operates as HM Prison Bure, a male category C prison.

RIGHT A calm day on the broads.

BELOW The view from the rising sun pub Coltishall.

The paddle

Both parking spots (see above) are right on the river with plenty of public launching nearby. Once on the water, turn right and head upstream for a couple of kilometres, passing lots of green space and some beautiful properties, including the Norfolk Mead hotel, where you will find the river splits in two.

You can go either way, but we highly recommend going left and following the quiet stretch of water through the trees until you find Horstead Mill (also known as the 'Bridge Over Water'). This is a beautiful mill pond – quiet and scenic. Following high periods of rain, the weir will be in full flow, so be sure to take extra caution as you get closer to the weir.

Once you've spent a moment enjoying the scenery, head out of the mill pond and very quickly there will be a narrow stretch of water on your left, which will take you out onto the main river. Turn left at the end of this passage and you'll come to a portage point, where you'll need to take your craft out and walk 50m to return to the water.

Once back on the water, continuing upstream, the river follows the tree lines, passing some local farmers' field and Hautbois Activity Centre for Girl Guides (this is a private site and there is no launching or access to the public).

The river then opens up and you can take in the beautiful views of Norfolk. Continue upriver alongside the Bure Valley Railway. This was a standard gauge railway until 1982, when the Broadland District Council decided to create a narrow gauge railway on the now defunct standard gauge, in order to fit a new pedestrian footpath alongside.

You will now pass under Mayton Bridge, a double-arch bridge which was built around 1630 and had to be repaired in 1984. Continue under the bridge, and soon you will pass under the railway and footpath bridge on your final approach to Buxton Mill.

When you see the river split, please keep to the left as it will take you to Buxton Mill.

This is the furthest point of the paddle, so enjoy the scenery here and maybe even go for a little dip in the water. Please note, the field on the left-hand side is private and restrictions may apply. Once ready, retrace your steps back to the start point in Coltishall.

Wildlife

On this route, you are likely to see swans, ducks, kingfishers, herons, fish and cattle. On a quiet day, you're bound to see even more, so be sure to keep an eye out.

COLTISHALL TO BUXTON MILL 121

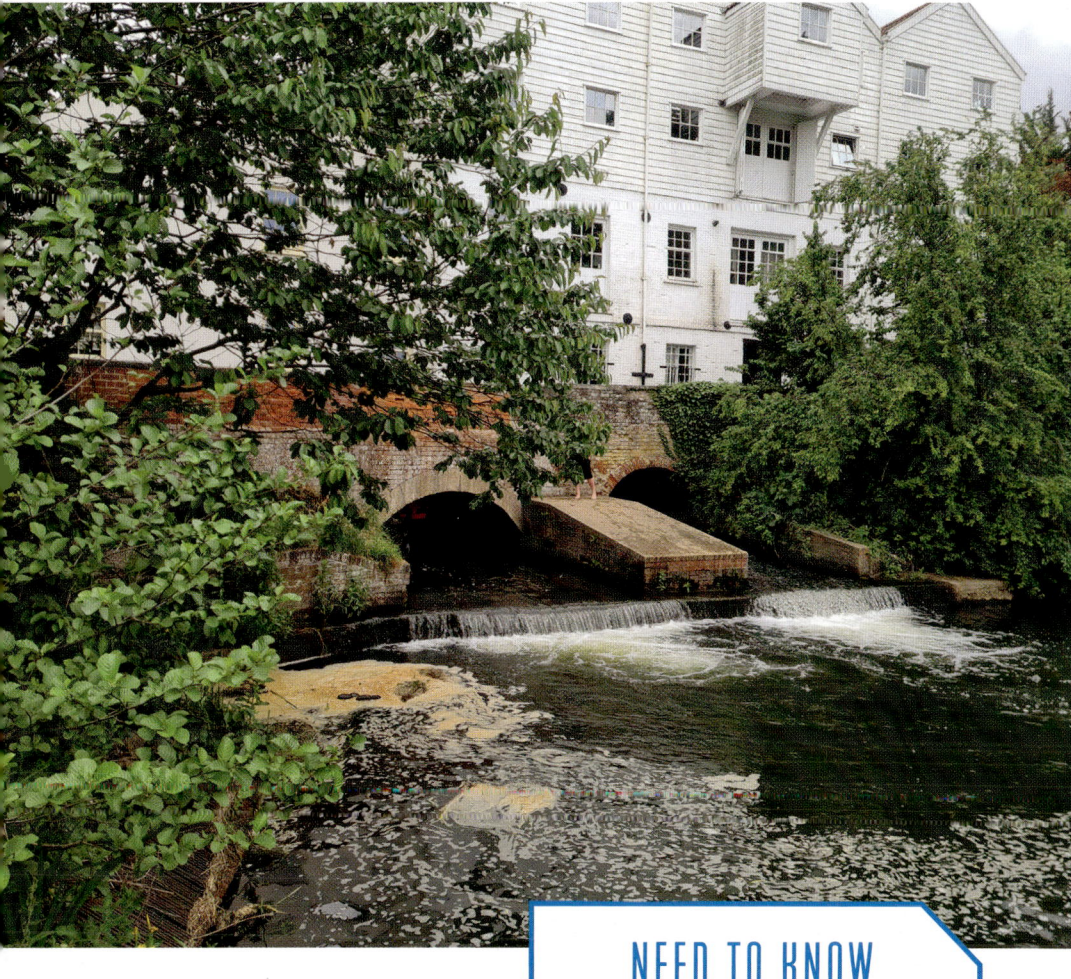

ABOVE Buxton Mill.

ABOVE LEFT Paddleboarders alongside the Bure Valley Railway.

Food stop
The Rising Sun pub (https://www.risingsubcoltishall.co.uk) is at the beginning of the paddle.

Other activities
There is canoe hire available next to the Rising Sun pub. You can also hire leisure boats in the nearby village of Wroxham. And if you've had your fill of the river, there are a number of public footpaths nearby.

NEED TO KNOW

■ You will require a Paddle UK or Broads Authority Licence for this paddle (see page 12 for more information).

■ Take extra caution if heading into the weir/mill pond.

■ The car park at Coltishall Common is busy in nice weather. The Rising Sun pub has alternative parking.

■ Be sure to observe any access restrictions along the route, e.g. for private fields.

22 ROCKLAND BROAD AND THE SLAUGHTERS

Part of the Broads National Park in Norfolk, Rockland Broad is around 20ha of water situated just off the River Yare, near to the village of Rockland St Mary. The Broad itself is surrounded by tall reedbeds and marshland. Hire craft and pleasure boats are restricted to two channels to and from the Broad (Short Dyke and Fleet Dyke) and within the Broad, while kayakers, canoeists and stand up paddleboarders can explore the entire Broad and surrounding area.

The Lowdown

DISTANCE 5km

WATER TYPE River and broad, slightly tidal

DIFFICULTY 💧

LICENCE REQUIRED ✓ (see Need to know box)

PARKING **Rockland Staithe** Rockland St Mary NR14 7HP, ///armful.handlebar.jogging. Free at time of writing. Approx. 30 spaces.

LAUNCH POINT NR14 7HP, ///token.media.polishing. From the car park it's only a few metres walk to the Staithe and launch point, a small concrete ramp next to the boat moorings for pleasure and hire craft. There's a locked gate but for a small donation the key can be obtained from The New Inn opposite (the key is in a small wooden box on the wall).

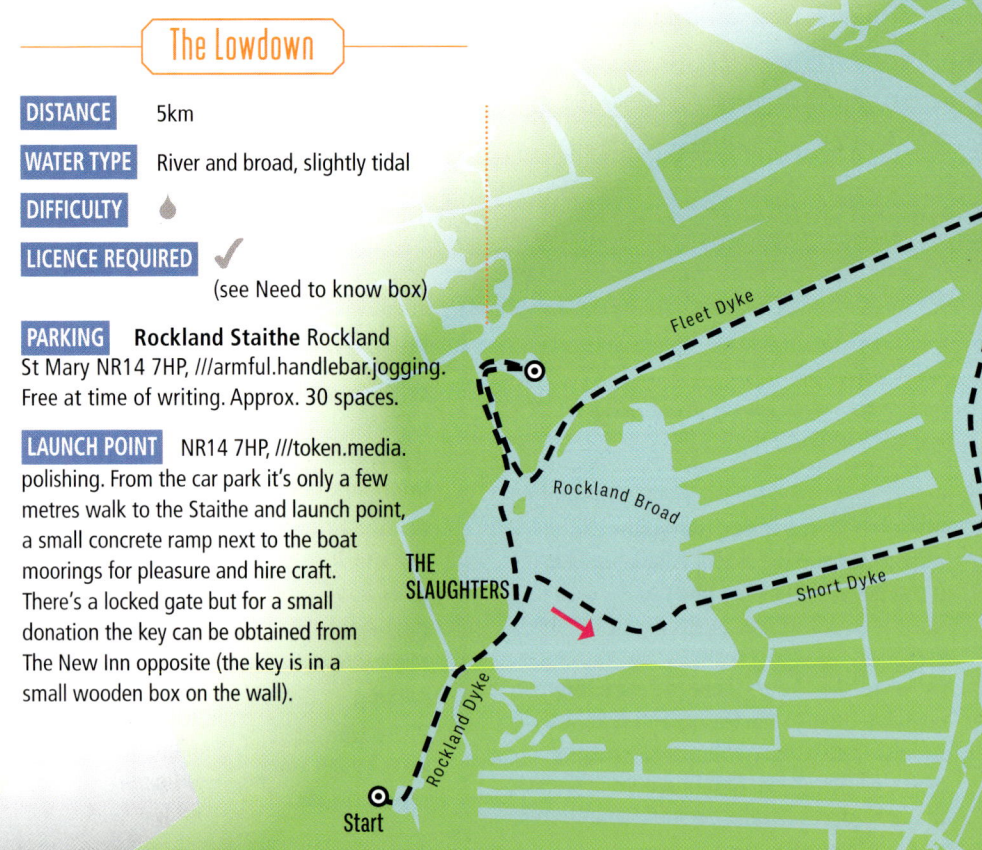

ROCKLAND BROAD AND THE SLAUGHTERS

ABOVE A mini island created by one of the Slaughters.

History

Probably the most notable historic feature of this Broad is 'The Slaughters', which sit on the western edge. Despite the scary name they are actually the remains of 13 or so Norfolk sailing wherries, gaff rigged clinker-built sailing boats with large black sails used to ferry cargo around the Broads in Norfolk and Suffolk. The wherries forming The Slaughters were sunk here in the mid 20th century as they came to the end of their commercial use. They have since become silted up and are now home to willow trees, other plants and wildlife. At low tide you can still see some of the timbers from the original boats, and if the water is clear you can see even more timbers and boat parts.

The paddle

Launch from a small concrete ramp next to the boat moorings for pleasure and hire craft (see above). Once launched, paddle north along Rockland Dyke, past the large Grand Designs-style black house on the right and then bear right into the main Broad, which opens up majestically in front of you. In the summer the area to your right outside of the main channel is a host of lily pads, which when in bloom are an amazing sight with a mass of yellow flowers.

The Slaughters are to your left as you enter the main Broad, and they line up along the western side, forming little islands to paddle around. They also separate one of the main channels from the western edge of the Broad and the RSPB Nature Reserve of Rockland Marsh.

To the north of the Broad is a nature reserve which, while being accessible to paddlers, has no landing points and can be quite overgrown, but nevertheless it is fun to explore.

There is plenty of water just for paddling and enjoying the views within the Broad, particularly to the south-east where there are areas roped off for nesting birds, and also the western side of The Slaughters.

If you would like a longer paddle, the loop around the dykes and River Yare is around 5km. Paddle along The Slaughters and roughly to the north you will see Fleet Dyke heading out of the Broad to the River Yare. Paddle to the end, past the boat moorings, and turn right. Follow the Yare until you see the next turn on your right: this is Short Dyke, which leads you back into the eastern end of Rockland Broad. There are points on Fleet and Short Dykes to and from the River Yare where you can sit on the moorings and enjoy a snack or picnic.

These dykes and the main river are used by pleasure and hire craft, so do take care and observe the keep right rule for paddling.

Wildlife

Lots of bird breeds make their home in Rockland, with 20 to 40 swans often seen here. Marsh harriers use it as their hunting ground and if you're lucky, one may pass low over your head. Kingfishers, with their distinctive flash of blue, can often be seen. In the reeds you can hear (and possibly see) reed warblers and chiffchaffs. On the main Broad, you may spot great crested grebes and shags fishing these waters.

The Broad is also known for good fishing, with many species, notably pike, bream, roach, tench and perch. There is a rumour that in 1912 a 31.5lb (14kg) pike was caught here.

Food stops

Opposite the launch at the Staithe is the New Inn, a traditional English pub serving hot and cold food and a great selection of drinks. Outside seating is right at the front of the pub.

Other activities

The Wherryman's Way, a 56km long-distance walking trail, passes right by Rockland on its way along the Yare Valley between Norwich and Great Yarmouth railways stations. Along this path at Rockland there is a bird hide overlooking the Broad, which is part of the RSPB Rockland Marshes Reserve.

NEED TO KNOW

■ A licence is required to paddle Rockland Broad, as it is for the entire Broads National Park (see page 12 for more information). Park rangers do actively check for licences.

■ Rockland Dyke, Fleet Dyke, Short Dyke and the River Yare are used by pleasure and hire craft so take care and observe the keep right rule for paddling.

■ There are no toilets or changing facilities other than the nearby pub, which is for customer use.

■ Dogs are welcome in the Broads National Park, but care should be taken around wildlife. Note, some nature reserves do not allow dogs.

TOP Lily pads in flower.

RIGHT Slaughters in a row, with the channel markers.

ROCKLAND BROAD AND THE SLAUGHTERS

23 NORWICH CITY PADDLE

Who would have thought a paddle through a city centre would be as lovely as this? Norwich is the only city in England within a national park: the River Wensum that flows through the city is part of the Broads National Park. And with Norwich being situated 160km north-east of London and 105km east of Peterborough, there are plenty of transport links to and from the city. This paddle takes place on the Yare, which soon becomes the River Wensum as you get further into the city. You start on the outskirts of the city and go past some historic sites before reaching the city.

The Lowdown

DISTANCE 14km
WATER TYPE River
DIFFICULTY ●●

LICENCE REQUIRED ✓ (see Need to know box)
PARKING ///punks.lime.robots
LAUNCH POINT **Grass Verge** which leads directly to the river. This is directly opposite the car park.///news.probe.little

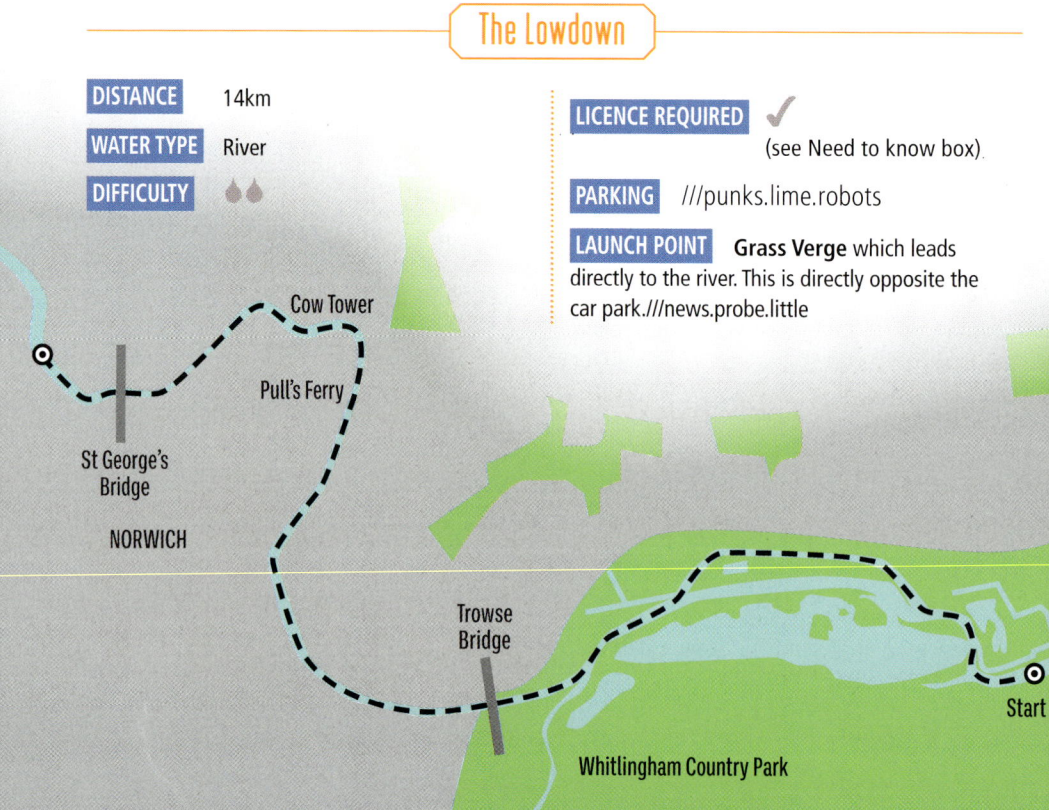

History

Norwich dates back to Roman times and is still today a very active city while maintaining its long history and culture. It is also claimed to be the most complete mediaeval city in the UK, and you'll pass by much of this long and storied history on this paddle.

By the Norman Conquest of 1066 Norwich was already established as a town, and the invading forces cleared the Saxon housing in the centre of the city to build a royal castle, assuming control of the town. Thirty years later, in 1096, the construction of the cathedral began. It took around 49 years to build, reaching completion in 1145. At 96m high, the cathedral spire is the second tallest in England (Salisbury's is taller, at 123m).

During mediaeval times Norwich went on to become England's second largest city, after London.

The paddle

After parking at Whitlingham Lane, put your craft onto the water and head left on the River Yare. Be mindful of the power craft on this stretch of water and remember to adhere to the waterways rules. Follow the river round and you'll find it splits into two. Going right under the railway bridge will take you past Thorpe Green.

Follow this stretch of water under the second railway bridge, where you will rejoin the main river.

Shortly after rejoining the river, you will go past Whitlingham Country Park on your left-hand side. As you pass the park, again the river will split into two. Heading left will take you by the canoe club and up to Racondale Mill, but for this paddle continue right. The river now becomes the Wensum.

Continue following the main river, and you will soon pass some vacant land on the left-hand side, which was previously used to unload wood deliveries used to make barrels for Colman's mustard.

You'll now come to the Trowse Bridge, a single-track railway bridge over the River Wensum, and the only swing bridge with an electrified line in the UK. On the left-hand side, make sure you look out for the old mill building with a white box on the front. Look closely as all the windows are faux! Further along, behind the flats on the right, you'll see Norwich City FC's stadium, Carrow Road. This stadium was built in just 82 days and opened on 31 August 1935.

You're now on the approach to Carrow Bridge. The two towers either side of the bridge were designed to protect the city from invasions, and the bridge now welcomes you to the city of Norwich.

Now you're in the city, you will pass under another couple of bridges: first up is Novi Sad Bridge, named after Norwich's twin town in former Yugoslavia, followed by Lady Julian Bridge, which was built in 2009 for £2.5 million. This bridge was named after a mediaeval mother, Julian, who wrote *Revelation of Divine Love* (1395), the first UK book written by a woman.

ABOVE Cow Tower.

By now you will be in the heart of the city, passing pubs, cinemas, shops, restaurants and Norwich train station. You'll also pass under Foundry Bridge, where you will find Norwich Yacht Station on the right. Continue past the station until you come to the historic landmark Pull's Ferry. This flint building is the former entrance to a canal accommodating the building of the cathedral in 1101.

You are now entering the historic part of the city, and you'll paddle under Bishop Bridge, built in 1340, making it one of the oldest bridges still in use, with great views of the cathedral on the left. Continue paddling straight and on the left-hand side you'll see the Cow Tower, one of the earliest purpose-built artillery block towers in England. It was built in about 1398 as an artillery base to defend the city, and is often known as the Black Tower. This is a good place to pull in and have a break. The shallow beach allows for great landing and there's a large green space where you can enjoy a picnic or a well-earned rest.

Once back on the water, continue left, past the Cow Tower. Continue until you reach the unique Jarrold Bridge, which is 80m long, bends round in the shape of a J and appears to float above the water. This bridge is next to the oldest pub in Norwich, the Adam and Eve. It is also known to be the last pub in Norwich

ABOVE Old railway bridge across the river.

which served ale from a barrel.

You are now approaching Whitefriars Bridge. Continue under the bridge and you'll see St James Mill, a textile mill built during the Industrial Revolution, on the right-hand side. As you paddle on, you'll pass the historic quayside, where not only will you see bright-coloured buildings but also blocks of wood, which bear traders' company and local names from the past.

Next up is Fye Bridge, Norwich's oldest-known bridge site, albeit it has since been rebuilt several times. The current structure was built in 1933 and stands in the same place as the original wooden structure. This bridge has plenty of history. Norwich was a centre during the witch trials of the 1600s, and the bridge was used to determine whether or not an accused women was practising witchcraft by dunking them into the river on a ducking stool.

Continue following the river past the Norwich University of Arts and under St George's Street Bridge. Next up is Dukes Palace Bridge, a former toll bridge located next to the Duke of Norfolk's residence.

You will now pass a building that appears to be covered in writing. This building was due to be demolished in 2000, so the artist Rory Macbeth painted the complete 4,000-

word work Thomas More's *Utopia*, published in 1516, across every brick.

Follow the river until you get to the mill, which is the turning point for this paddle. If you still have time and/or energy, you can portage past the mill and continue on to Hellesdon Mill, a lovely part of the Wensum.

Wildlife

There are many opportunities to see a huge variety of birdlife on the river, including Egyptian and Canadian geese, mallards, swans and Cayuga ducks (black with a green sheen). As you paddle on through the city, you may also see herons, kingfishers, grey wagtails and cormorants.

Food stops

With this paddle going through the heart of the city which once had 600 pubs, there are many options for finding something suitable to eat and drink. Many of the pubs on this route have slipways and pontoons, making them easily accessible to people arriving by all types of crafts.

Other activities

Norwich is within the Broads National Park, making this a fantastic hopping off points to explore everything the park has to offer, including boat hire (both day and overnight are available).

ABOVE Kayak paddling down the River Wensum.
OVERLEAF Pulls Ferry Flint.

The Norfolk Broads contain over 300km of footpath and trails, so there's plenty of ways to explore the beautiful sites on foot. You also have rail access to explore many of the areas covered in this book.

There is also plenty to do in the city, with the high street and city attractions nearby. The Norwich Riverside and Cathedral Quarter Walk is a short circular walk that takes you alongside the River Wensum and around the cathedral grounds, including past many of the historic sites mentioned in this chapter.

NEED TO KNOW

■ Although the Wensum is a tidal river, you will require a Paddle UK or Broads Authority Licence to paddle here (see page 12 for more information).

■ The launch point can be steep if there is a low tide.

■ This route can be popular with leisure craft, so proceed with caution and observe the keep right rule of paddling.

24 SURLINGHAM BROAD AND BARGATE

Surlingham Broad, in the Broads National Park, is small and secluded, with an open 7.5ha area of water known as Bargate. Surlingham Broad, in the Broads National Park, is small and secluded, with an open 7.5ha area of water known as Bargate. It is situated just off the southern edge of the River Yare as it passes between the pretty villages of Brundle and Surlingham among 80ha of marshland.

The Lowdown

DISTANCE 12km

WATER TYPE River and Broad, slightly tidal

DIFFICULTY 💧💧

LICENCE REQUIRED ✓ (see Need to know box)

PARKING **Rockland Staithe** Rockland St Mary NR14 7HP, ///armful.handlebar.jogging. Free at time of writing. Approx. 30 spaces.

LAUNCH POINT NR14 7HP, ///token.media.polishing. From the car park it is only a few metres walk to the Staithe and launch point, a small concrete ramp next to the boat moorings for pleasure and hire craft. There's a locked gate but for a small donation the key can be obtained from The New Inn opposite (the key is in a small wooden box on the wall).

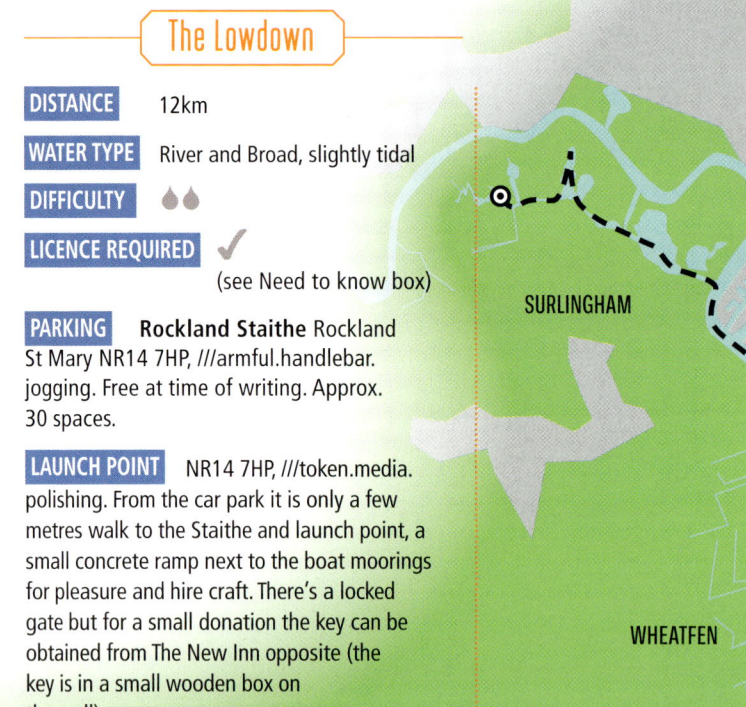

SURLINGHAM BROAD AND BARGATE

The Broad is surrounded by tall reedbeds and trees and can be divided into three parts: first is two channels to and from the River Yare known as Bird's Dyke and Surlingham Fleet; second is the small open area called Bargate; and third is the twisty secluded area full of tiny channels and ponds, such as Bunney's Broad and Newman's Hole, open only to small paddlecraft. Hire craft and pleasure boats are restricted to the two channels and within Bargate, while kayakers, canoeists and stand up paddleboarders can explore the entire Broad and surrounding area.

History
Surlingham Broad has two claims to fame. First, British botanist and ecologist Joyce Lambert studied this area, leading to the conclusion that the Broads and 'lakes' within them were in fact, contrary to previous publications, humanmade. Her research, which centred on removing core samples of peat with a borer, proved that the Broads were a result of peat digging, with the sides of many of the 'lakes' being vertical. This practice ceased in the 1400s due to flooding caused by rising sea and water levels and a deterioration of the local climate.

Second, Surlingham Broad is home to Harbrough's Graveyard, a chained-off bay on the eastern side of Bargate which contains 13 Norfolk sailing wherries that were sunk here at the end of their working life. You can still see many of their timbers protruding from the water.

The paddle
Once launched, paddle along Rockland Dyke, bear left into Rockland Broad and head roughly to the north and into Fleet Dyke heading out of the Broad

BELOW The sign to watch for on the left at the entrance to Surlingham Fleet.

to the River Yare. As you reach the main river, turn left again. You are now paddling between two nature reserves, Wheaten Fen to your left and Strumpshaw Fen and the Mid-Yare National Nature Reserve to your right.

You soon start to see a large marina on your right, which is the start of the village of Brundall, and on your left a very nice thatched-roof building, which is Coldham Hall Tavern. Built in the early 1800s and since extended, it's a nice place to stop for a drink and some good food.

Next door to the pub is a boatyard and the remains of a former 'wherry slip', which was once used to launch and recover Norfolk sailing wherries. The next turn on the left is the entrance to the Broad known as Surlingham Fleet (see photo on page 135).

A short paddle along the Fleet and Bargate opens up into a small open area where some pleasure craft moor for the night. Immediately on your right is the chained-off area of Harbrough's Graveyard and the sunken wherries. The western end of Bargate is Fleet Dyke, which turns right and heads back out to the River Yare. Here, small unpowered draft can continue west into the labyrinth that is the main part of Surlingham Broad. Care should be taken not to get lost here: there are many small channels and openings, but it is an incredible experience to explore such an unspoilt area. Some parts are named locally, such as King's Fleet and Moore's Water. As the seasons change and the trees and rushes grow and recede, this area changes, too, with channels opening and closing, so a few trips here are recommended.

Returning through this natural maze to Bargate and back along the route to the launch completes your paddle.

BELOW The River Ranger in Surlingham Fleet after checking our licences.

Wildlife

The Norfolk Broads is a hunting ground for marsh harriers and if you're lucky one may pass low over your head. Kingfishers, with their distinctive flash of blue, can often be seen here. In the reeds you can hear (and possibly see) reed warblers and chiffchaffs.

Food stops

Opposite the launch at the Staithe is The New Inn, a traditional English pub serving hot and cold food and a great selection of drinks. Outside seating is right at the front of the pub.

Coldham Hall Tavern is along the route, and other local pubs and cafés are available in Surlingham village.

Other activities

Wheaten Fen is paddled past on this route and is one of the most significant and well-studied wetland nature reserves in Britain. Spanning 52ha, it consists of large swathes of open fen, reedbeds and a network of pathways that are open to the public to explore.

BELOW Swans and part of a wherry near the chains.
OVERLEAF In the maze of the Broad.

NEED TO KNOW

■ A licence is required to paddle Rockland Broad, as it is for the entire Broads National Park (see page 12 for more information). Park rangers do actively check for licences.

■ Most of this paddle is on sections also used by pleasure and hire craft, so take care and observe the keep right rule for paddling.

■ The main attraction of Surlingham is the maze of channels and ponds. Care should be taken to avoid getting lost, and you will need a means of navigation. Loading Google Maps on your phone (and carrying it in a waterproof case!) is ideal, or for a more traditional method, tie ribbons to trees and recover them as you return.

■ There are no toilets or changing facilities other than the nearby pub, which is for customer use.

■ Dogs are welcome in the Broads National Parks, but be cautious around wildlife.

25 BUNGAY LOOP

The Bungay Loop is not actually a loop, but more horseshoe-shaped as an out-and-back paddle around Outney Common. The loop is part of the River Waveney, which runs from Lopham Fenn to the coast at Great Yarmouth via Oulton Broad and forms the boundary between Suffolk and Norfolk.

The Lowdown

DISTANCE 7–8km

WATER TYPE River

DIFFICULTY 💧

LICENCE REQUIRED ✓
(see Need to know box)

PARKING **Outney Meadow Caravan Park** Bungay NR35 1HG, ///reefs.accordian.lobbed. £5–£10 for the day, depending on craft. Due to recent parking restrictions, the free parking at Bungay Staithe is no longer available.

LAUNCH POINT Launch is close to the Outney Meadow car park (above) and a short walk through the campsite, ///fade.lyricism.distorts.

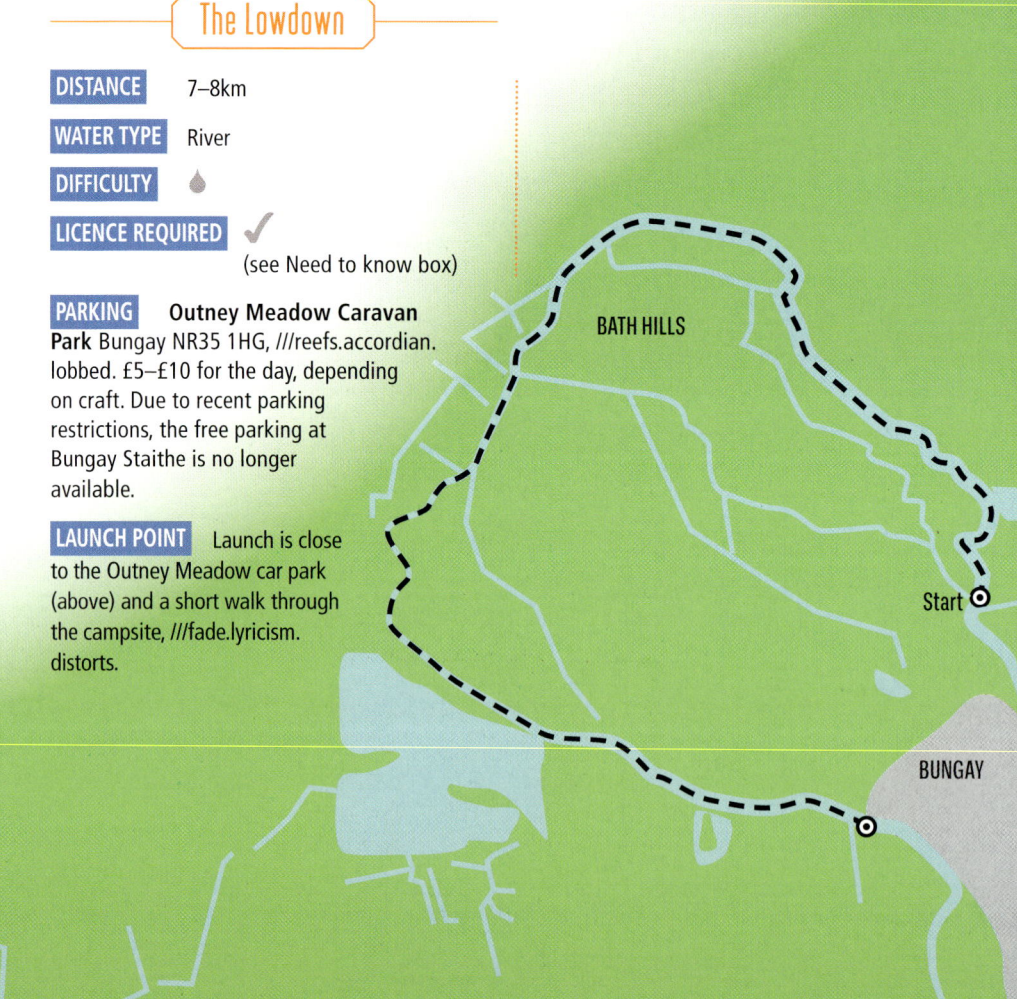

History

Bungay is a historic market town in the heart of the Waveney Valley. It sits at the head of navigation on the River Waveney and the loop, an ox-bow meander, is probably the furthest you can paddle easily towards the source of the river. The loop leaves the village and passes through farmland and around the long-established Bungay & Waveney Valley golf course, with both ends of the loop alongside the A143 major road.

Bungay has a rich trading history, including paper manufacture and more recently brewing. It is also a town of myths and legends, including The Black Dog, a large black Hell Hound that appeared in 1577 following a thunderstorm and lightning strike on the village church, although it has not seen since the 1800s…

The paddle

Launching from the campsite pontoon, paddle upstream to the left and you'll shortly see some open farmland and a fork in the river. The left-hand channel is known as the Old River and is the original path of the river, but you need to take the right-hand fork to continue this loop.

After passing more farmland and a couple of bends in the river you'll reach a small island to your right and another fork in the river. The right-hand fork can be passable at times, although very shallow and overgrown. The left fork passes under a footbridge and continues along the river,

ABOVE Paddling under the footbridge in the rain.

BELOW Cows joining the river for a drink.

rejoining the right fork at the end of the island, where there is sometimes a rope swing from the large tree. The paddle now passes between farmland on your right and Ditchingham Lodge on your left, a Grade II listed building built in the mid-1800s.

The river starts to meander to the right around the Bath Hills on your right and woodland to your left, passing Wood House, Cold Bath House and Bath Hills Farm. It is said that in the 1930s a flying circus would visit the hills, offering flying trips for 5 shillings.

At this point you're roughly halfway around the loop, and you'll be able to catch a glimpse of Bungay town to your right, before passing between the golf course, which has been here in various forms since 1889, and a family-run quarry, operating since 1949. You may also hear the boats on the lake at the Waveney Water Ski Club, on the left-hand side of the river.

The last stretch of river is surrounded by trees and woodland and is a favourite of fishermen. As you reach the A143 road bridge the river narrows, shallows and the flow increases, signalling the end of the loop.

Return to the launch by simply retracing your steps to the campsite. If you want a longer paddle, continue past here towards the charming town of Beccles via a portage at the Bungay Staithe Weir.

Wildlife

The meadow you paddle around has shared ownership, and the owners have the right to graze sheep and cows, which are often seen drinking from, or even in, the river as you pass.

The water on this stretch or the river is very clear, allowing you to see rudd, perch, bream, pike and tench, and you may even spot freshwater mussels.

Kingfishers dart along the surface of the water, while swans breed here and you may even spot a heron. In the summer yellow water lilies add colour along with butterflies and damselflies.

Bats and owls are often seen in the evening hunting. If you're very lucky you may even see the otters that live here.

Food stops

There are no food stops and very limited landings on this loop, so pack a picnic to eat on the water, or plan to visit one of the many local pubs or cafés, either in Bungay or the adjacent village of Ditchingham. The Green Dragon in Bungay is not only a nice pub serving good food but it also has an on-site brewery serving its own beer, and is just a short walk from the campsite.

Other activities

The area has many churches and castles to visit including the Norman castle Bigod, which was built in 1100 by Roger Bigod and adapted over the centuries. It also gives name to the Bigod Way, a 5.5km circular walk around the Bungay, Ditchingham and Earsham, part of which follows this paddle's loop. You can also add another 8km and take in the historic villages of St John Ilketshall and Mettingham.

NEED TO KNOW

- A Waterways Licence is required for this stretch of water (see page 12 for more information). Paddle UK offers good value membership, which includes access to the water, third party public liability insurance and various discounts nationwide.

- The northern side of the river is almost all private land, so there are very limited options for landing and stopping on the loop.

TOP A rainy paddle on the loop.

ABOVE Sheltering from the rain on the loop.

CAMBRIDGESHIRE

Where ancient fens meet academic brilliance and watery adventures.

In England's east lies Cambridgeshire, a county where history and innovation intertwine. A land shaped by the ebb and flow of the Fens, it offers a unique blend of natural beauty, cultural richness, academic prowess and exhilarating water-based adventures.

The Fens, a vast wetland reclaimed over centuries, form the heart of Cambridgeshire. This tranquil expanse is not only home to a diverse array of wildlife but also a paradise for paddlers. Explore the serene waterways by canoe, kayak, or stand up paddleboard, immersing yourself in the natural beauty of this unique landscape.

Cambridgeshire's intellectual heritage is renowned worldwide. The University of Cambridge, one of the world's leading academic institutions, has called this region home for centuries. Its iconic architecture and vibrant student life infuse the city with energy and inspiration. Beyond Cambridge, the county is dotted with charming market towns, each with its own distinct character.

History lovers will find themselves immersed in a world of discovery. From the Roman era to the mediaeval period, Cambridgeshire has played a significant role in shaping England. Explore the majestic Ely Cathedral, a masterpiece of Norman architecture, or wander through the historic streets of Huntingdon and St Ives.

Whether you seek academic inspiration, outdoor adventure on the water or a journey through time, Cambridgeshire offers an unforgettable experience!

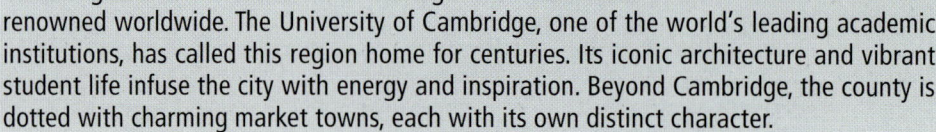

TOP Paddling under the Bridge of Sighs.

RIGHT Paddling in Cambridge.

26 ELY – RIVER GREAT OUSE

Ely, England's second smallest city with a population of 15,000, is situated on the River Great Ouse in Cambridgeshire. The river is the fifth longest river in the UK, and flows through Buckinghamshire, Bedfordshire, Cambridgeshire and Norfolk before draining into The Wash and North Sea near King's Lynn for a total distance of 225–257km and 18 locks. As with most of the rivers in the UK, it was historically used for commercial navigation, but these days is mainly populated by pleasure craft including canal boats, motorboats, rowers and paddleboarders.

The Lowdown

- **DISTANCE** 1–17km
- **WATER TYPE** River
- **DIFFICULTY** 💧
- **LICENCE REQUIRED** ✓ (see Need to know box)
- **PARKING** Fisherman's 34 Willow Walk, Ely CB7 4EB, ///bottom.bulbs.moving. Free long-stay car park, though 90 min max, between 8am and 8.30am. Ely train station is also situated next to the river.
- **LAUNCH POINT** End of car park (see above), towards the river by Pegasus walk, ///lifetimes.jazz.today. You'll see a concrete edge where you can launch from, but take care, as during the dry season this can be a bit of a drop.

RIGHT Ely Cathedral.

History

The city of Ely occupies the largest island in the Cambridgeshire Fens – the 'Isle of Ely', which was only accessible by boat until the waterlogged Fens was drained in the 17th century. This is how Ely got its name: the Anglo-Saxons called it Eilig, or the 'Isle of Eels'.

Ely was founded by an Anglo-Saxon princess, St Etheldreda, who founded the Christian community on top of the island hills in AD 673. The Anglo-Saxon church has not survived, but from these hills you can see the magnificent Norman cathedral, towering over the Fens. The cathedral took 300 years to complete and it still stands just as majestically 1,000 years later.

The paddle

Launch from the car park. You can head either way on the river depending on your destination. Heading right of the launch point takes you through Ely towards Little Thetford, while if you turn left you'll paddle towards Littleport.

ABOVE Canal boats on the main stretch through Ely.

RIGHT The trainline running above the River Great Ouse near the launch site.

Paddling to the right through Ely itself is a short paddle equating to 1.9km from the launch point to the end of the city; however there are plenty of pubs and restaurants to stop at to extend the trip. And should you wish to explore more of the River Great Ouse, you can paddle further towards the direction of Little Thetford and into the countryside that surrounds the area (9.7km return). There are some magnificent canal boats to see on this little stretch too.

If you paddle to the left to Littleport, you'll pass Ely Country Park and the Roswell Pits Nature Reserve on your left. It's an 8km paddle to Littleport, which is part of the Fens, so you'll notice how flat the surroundings are and, depending on the time of year, you may also observe that the soil in this area is very dark peaty soil. The trainline runs alongside this stretch of the river.

Wildlife

As many as 70,000 critically endangered European eels make the long journey up the River Great Ouse from the Sargasso Sea over the course of two years. They then spend up to 20 years living in the river before they reach maturity and head back to the Sargasso Sea to spawn. However, they are secretive, generally nocturnal creatures, so you'll be lucky to spot them.

As there is a nature reserve in Ely, there is plentiful wildlife, with the surrounding area providing an array of welcoming, including lakes, reedbeds, seasonally flooded meadows, woodlands and grasslands. This variety means a wealth of different species can be found here, such as water voles, otters, bats and a variety of plants including the bee orchid. Birds include swans, coots, moorhens and tawny owls. Even red squirrels have been spotted in the area!

Roswell Pits also provides a fantastic habitat for breeding birds such as the great crested grebe, tufted duck and kingfisher.

ELY – RIVER GREAT OUSE

It has plentiful foraging and resting areas for overwintering birds, too, including the bittern.

Food stops

There are several restaurants, tearooms, cafés and pubs along the river, while the city centre is only a short walk away. Peacocks is an award-winning, family-owned deli and tearoom situated alongside the river, behind Babylon Arts: www.peacockstearoom.co.uk/.

Other activities

The main attraction in Ely is the cathedral. The cathedral can be seen from miles around, sitting on the hill surrounded by the flat landscape of the Fens. Visitors will also find a stained-glass museum situated inside, beautiful green spaces and gardens and various guided tours: www.elycathedral.org/. A market is also situated near the cathedral, as well as various shops, cafés and restaurants.

There is plentiful history to be found around this small city and various museums and historical landmarks,

including the former family home of Oliver Cromwell, which also houses a Civil War exhibition with interactive displays: www.olivercromwellshouse.co.uk/.

Babylon Arts, the leading arts authority in Ely, is situated alongside the river and includes a gallery, cinema and live dance and drama. Admission is free and they often have free art activities for visitors: www.babylonarts.org.uk/.

There are various boat hire companies along the river, and you can even rent canal boats as bed and breakfasts.

Ely Country Park is situated at the other end of Fisherman's car park, with plenty of lovely walks, and playgrounds and obstacles for the kids. Roswell Pits Nature Reserve is just a little further down along the river.

The best way to see Ely is to walk. There are guided tours and walks around the city but there are also various routes and trails you can walk on your own, such as the Ely Circular Trail and the Ely Cathedral and

ABOVE Trainline Bridge over the river.

RIGHT Beautiful canal boats moored up along the river.

River Trail. More information is easily accessible online and displayed around the city.

NEED TO KNOW

■ A Waterways Licence is required for this stretch of water (see page 12 for more information). Paddle UK offers good value membership, which includes access to the water, third party public liability insurance and various discounts nationwide.

■ This stretch of river is frequented by pleasure craft, so take care and observe the keep right rule for paddling.

27 CAMBRIDGE – THE BACKS

One of the country's most iconic paddles, this stretch of the Cam meanders through the beautiful city of Cambridge, famed the world over for its historic university. You'll paddle by some of the university's oldest colleges, under some of the oldest and most elegant bridges, and some very well-looked-after green lawns!

This area can be exceptionally busy through the summer months, with tourists taking a ride on one of the many punts operating in the area, so do bear this in mind when planning your trip.

The Lowdown

DISTANCE 2.5km/5km

WATER TYPE River

DIFFICULTY

LICENCE REQUIRED ✓ (see Need to know box)

PARKING **Lammas Land** The Driftway, Newnham Rd, Cambridge CB3 9JJ, ///dress.bands.navy. Pay and display at time of writing. Nearby facilities, including a kids' play area and paddling pool. Approx. 75 spaces, including 4 disabled spaces. Height barrier 1.98m.

LAUNCH POINT From the car park (above), you'll see a launch area, ///minin.snows.decks. Please be considerate not to block the footpath as this can be quite a busy area.

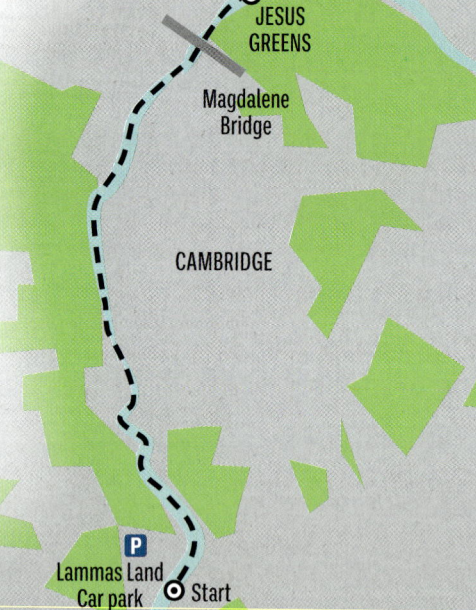

CAMBRIDGE – THE BACKS

ABOVE Paddling towards the Mathematical Bridge.

OVERLEAF Paddling past Kings College.

History

The River Cam is one of very few rivers in England to be named after the town it runs through – the original name, 'River Granta', is still used in some areas. The river flows from its sources in Debden, Essex and Ashwell, Hertfordshire, to the sea at King's Lynn in Norfolk via the Great Ouse. The Cam has around 25 bridges. On this paddle through The Backs, you will see 10 – all within roughly 1.6km! Arguably some are nicer to look at and are more famous than others, while some are more famous: for example, Magdalen Bridge, located on Bridge Street, is the bridge that gave the city its name – 'Cam-Bridge'.

The paddle

Once launched, you need to paddle to the right. You'll then quickly see a junction in the river, where you should paddle left. This takes you past the Cambridge Canoe Club, under the Fen Causeway road bridge, then under Crusoe Bridge, the first named bridge of your paddle, and last before your portage towards the famous city sights!

Once you have eyes on the Graduate Hilton hotel, you'll see the portage on the left. Enter the water via the slipway, alongside the floodgates. This is known as Mill Pond. Many of the punting tours start from here, so it can be very busy! You'll then pass under Silver Street Bridge, next to The Anchor pub. On your left is Queens' College. You'll paddle under the Mathematical Bridge, a unique wooden structure that connects two parts of the college. Next up you'll see three archways across the water: King's College Bridge, Clare Bridge

(the oldest on the River Cam, built in 1639) and Trinity Bridge. On your right now is the stunning King's College. It is worth pausing here to take in the views.

When you are ready to continue, carry on in the same direction, which will take you past the Wren Library building. Around the corner, you will paddle under Kitchen Bridge, and then to the most photographed bridge of this trip, the Grade I listed Bridge of Sighs – designed and based on a similarly named bridge in Venice, although the only real similarity between the two is they're both covered bridges over waterways. The last bridge on this paddle is known as Magdalene Bridge, located next to Magdalene College. From here, you will see the Quayside, with lots of bars and restaurants – you can take a break here, though do be mindful of where you leave your kit, as Scudamore's Quayside Punting Station is based here and operates daily. Just a few hundred metres ahead is Jesus Lock and Jesus Green. This is a nice spot to take a break, with lots of open space, and it marks the end of this paddle. Turn around here and paddle back to Lammas Land car park. The return journey offers different views of the city; keep your eyes peeled

LEFT Paddling towards Kings College.
BELOW Paddling towards Kitchen Bridge.

for St John's College, which boasts the largest ivy wall in the UK, at over 180 years old! Standing up gives a better viewpoint along the river, with those low down often missing views of the college buildings, so a paddleboard would be ideal for this trip.

Food stops

There are many places to stop on this paddle, whether you bring a packed lunch and enjoy it on the riverbank with stunning views, or pause to eat at a pub or restaurant. The Graduate and The Anchor (previously mentioned) are located in the earlier stages of the paddle, so either would make a nice return treat. Café Foy in the Quayside has nice outside seating for smaller groups, and there are numerous other eateries in the area.

Wildlife

Ducks, swans and moorhens are a common sight along the river, but you might also see the occasional kingfisher in quieter areas. Very rare sightings of black swans, Egyptian geese and Mandarin ducks have been reported, all of which have likely escaped from bird collections. Due to the popularity of this stretch, wildlife is limited. The river hosts usual the fish species, including roach, bream, pike; however fishing isn't popular here.

Other activities

Cambridge is a fascinating city, with lots of history. There are plenty of walks around the city and along the river, taking in world-class museums, libraries and botanic gardens. Jesus Green Lido is one of Europe's largest open-air swimming pools; and is of course very popular in the summer months: www.cambridge.gov.uk/jesus-green-lido.

A visit to the city wouldn't be complete without a trip along the water, whether that be via paddling or on a punt – a long, narrow, flat-bottomed boat, operated using a traditional pole. You can hire these yourself or take a chauffeured trip, allowing you to take in all the views.

In 2018, East of England Paddlesports joined up with other providers and attended a Santa Paddle on the Cam, with around 100 festive-themed paddlers taking to the water to raise money for Cancer Research. However, due to the success of our group, and limited parking, we have stopped going to this area as much as we would like, as any sizeable groups need to register their event with the River Cam Conservancy.

NEED TO KNOW

■ A Waterways Licence is required for this stretch of water. Paddle UK offers the best value membership, and the 'on the water' membership includes access to the Cam. The Cam Conservancy requires your licence number to be on display from your chosen craft at all times (see page 12 for more information).

■ Sizeable groups need to register their event with the River Cam Conservancy.

■ This area can be extremely busy. Please adhere to navigational rules and adhere to the keep right rule for paddling.

RIGHT Paddling under the Bridge of Sighs.
BELOW Boston Ivy Wall on St Johns College.

BEDFORDSHIRE

Open a map of England, and nestled amidst the southern counties lies Bedfordshire, a place where time seems to weave a delightful tapestry. This charming county offers a captivating blend of history and natural beauty, all intertwined with the lifeblood of the region – the River Great Ouse.

Bedfordshire boasts a rich heritage, evident in its grand country estates like Woburn Abbey, whispering tales of aristocratic families. Wander through the ruins of Dunstable Priory, once a powerful monastery, or explore the Iron Age hillforts that crown the Chiltern Hills, silent sentinels standing guard over centuries.

Escape the hustle and bustle and delve into Bedfordshire's idyllic countryside. Traverse the chalk downlands of Dunstable Downs, a designated National Landscape, and soak in panoramic vistas. Follow tranquil trails through the Marston Vale Community Forest, a haven for diverse wildlife, or explore the hidden gems like Sharpenhoe Clappers, a Bronze Age monument shrouded in mystery.

The River Great Ouse snakes its way majestically through Bedfordshire, its waters a vital artery for both nature and history. Often described as the "Jewel in the Crown" of Bedford, the county town, the Ouse has powered mills, provided a trade route to the North Sea for centuries, and served as a source of recreation for generations. Today, the riverbanks offer a delightful escape, perfect for a leisurely stroll or a scenic bike ride. Take a trip along the calm waters, a quintessential English experience, and admire the verdant landscapes that fringe the river.

Bedfordshire offers something for every visitor. So, lace up your walking boots, delve into its intriguing past, or simply relax amidst the tranquillity of the rolling English countryside, all while enjoying the timeless beauty of the River Great Ouse.

TOP Colourful Tulips that line the river.

RIGHT Aerial shot of Bedford Top River.

28 KEMPSTON TO BEDFORD TOWN CENTRE & TOP RIVER

The Great Ouse is a heavyweight among English rivers, clocking in at around 225–257km long! It starts its journey in Northamptonshire, winds its way through several counties and finally empties into the North Sea near King's Lynn. The Great Ouse is a river that can cater for all abilities, with faster flowing stretches for the more experienced, to slower, wider sections for all to enjoy. You can experience nature at its finest in some of the wilder sections, or embark on an urban paddle through the town centre.

The Lowdown

DISTANCE 4km/1.8km

WATER TYPE River

DIFFICULTY

LICENCE REQUIRED
(see Need to know box)

PARKING **Kempston: Mill Lane** Kempston, Bedford MK42 7BD, ///shrug.brochure.lower. Free at time of writing. Approx. 12 spaces. Road parking also possible close by – please check local restrictions.
Top River: Prebend Mill Meadows MK42 0BQ, ///leads.dive.bridge. Either walk across the bridge to reach the scenic Top River or paddle the bottom river to a portage point before crossing into the top section. Free road parking also available along Embankment east end, close to river. Check road signage for local restrictions

LAUNCH POINT Kempston ///ranked.brink.craters. When launching, please avoid the weir upstream (to the left) of the launch. This is notably quite a dangerous weir.
Top River ///fails.intro.noble. Access easily available from the bank along the road.

History

Bedford is a historic market town on the River Great Ouse, situated on the arc between Oxford and Cambridge. It began life as a Saxon village, due to its location as an excellent river crossing point.

The river cuts through the Fens, a historically marshy region. Over time, clever engineering projects have been put in place to drain the land using the Ouse, making it more farmable. Over the centuries, Bedford became an important market town. Vikings even raided it, but the English fought back and built a castle (which is mostly gone now). Bedford used to be famous for making wool and lace, but today it has a mixture of businesses. The town still has a lovely old centre with some reminders of its history, like a big church and a castle mound.

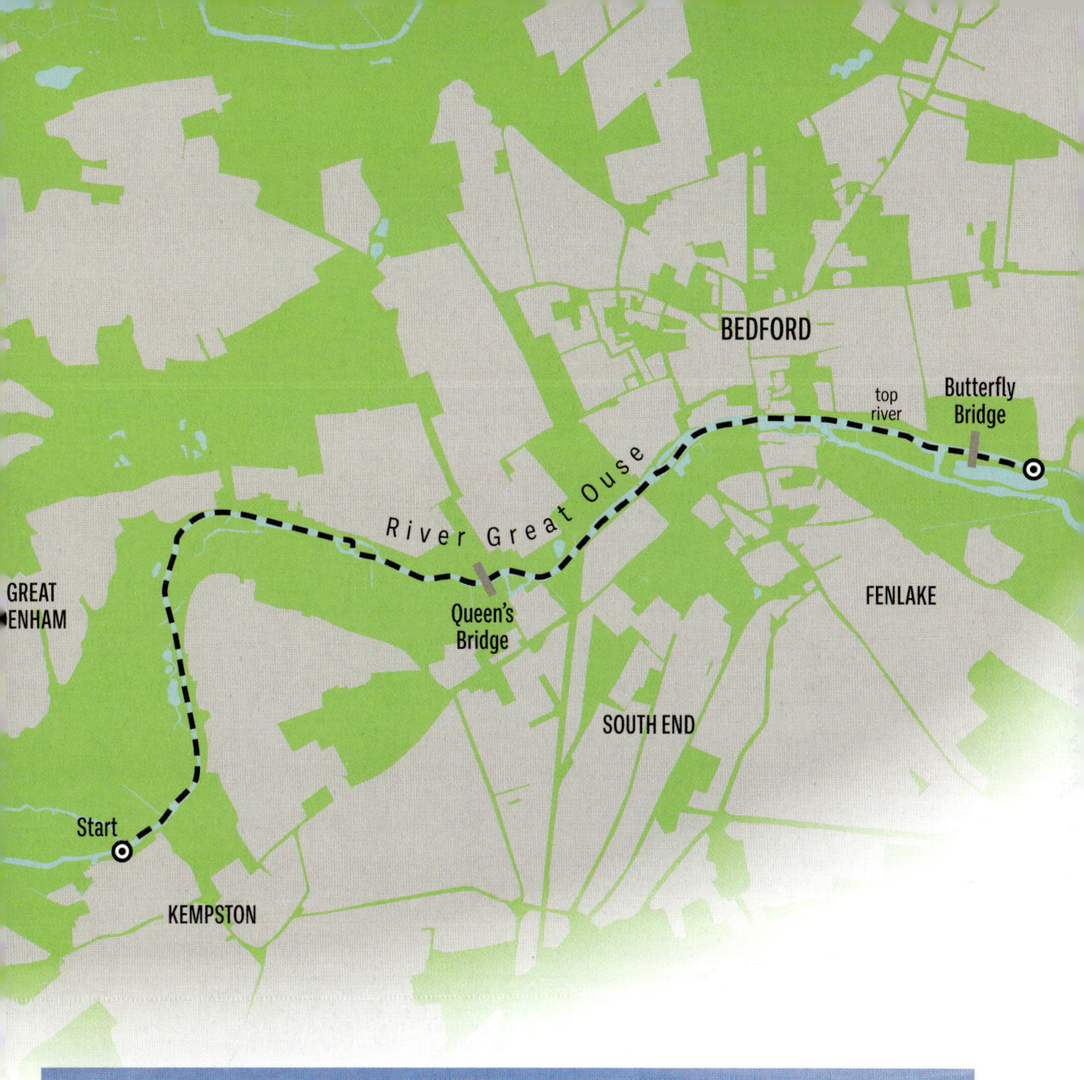

ABOVE Blue sky paddles at Kempston Mill.

Canoeist Etienne Stott, who trained in Bedford, is an Olympic champion, winning gold in the C2 canoe slalom at the London 2012 Summer Olympics. The Duckmill Weir White Water Area was renamed the Etienne Stott Arena in tribute to the champion, with slalom poles and controlled jets installed as a permanent fixture the same year.

The paddle

When you launch in Kempston, head downstream, paddle past a small island and stick to the left channel. Follow the river down past the Great Denham Nature Reserve. Keep paddling and you'll get to a squeeze, where the trees encroach onto the river. Make your way through and soon you'll approach Honey Hill Islands – keep an eye for the signs pointing you towards the right channel and paddle through here, being mindful of low-hanging trees and debris, and the occasional fisherman, who often frequent the banks here. Carry on here and the river opens up. You'll soon arrive at the picturesque footbridge Queens Bridge. Paddle under and carry on. The river gets even wider here so be mindful of the winds if they pick up.

Keep going, and you'll soon paddle under two low train bridges. To the left you'll see some slalom poles hanging from the bridge, which have been set up by the local Viking Kayak Club. If you fancy a go, try and get through without touching any of the poles! Carry on and you'll pass under a suspension footbridge, followed quickly by another train bridge and then a road bridge. As you approach the road bridge, decide if you'll continue on the right-hand side, which is the main open stretch of river, or left of the island, where you can pause for a break before the private jetties that belong to Star Rowing Club and the before mentioned Viking club. If you wanted to start your paddle here, please contact the club to arrange a day membership, which includes

ABOVE AND LEFT The Butterfly Bridge.

parking, access to facilities, launching and insurance (if you don't already hold a Waterways Licence). Alternatively, there is a car park on the opposite side of the river called Prebend Street (please check restrictions here). It's a short walk across the bridge to launch from the public mooring.

If pausing here, you can find public facilities and food options in the town centre. This is also a good turning point if you wanted a shorter paddle – it's 4km to this point, so 8km there and back. To extend your paddle, you can continue on the same route, which will take you through Bedford town centre into an area also known as 'Top River'.

Top River At roughly 1.8km, this stretch is considered the most popular part of the River Great Ouse, with public parks, war memorials, riverside gardens, boating lake and cafés along the route. If paddling the full stretch, you'll paddle under several bridges, including the suspension bridge, and the iconic Butterfly Bridge. Lots of other river users, including rowing boats (of which there are three clubs along this short stretch), canal boats and motorised boats will be operating here, especially through the summer months. Every year, usually in July, Bedford Borough Council holds a river festival, which is said to be the second largest free festival in the country.

Wildlife The River Great Ouse is full of life! Depending on where you paddle, look out for fish like perch and pike swimming around. Colourful kingfishers zoom by, while herons stand tall on the edge of the river. You might even see otters playing in the water, or deer coming for a drink. As is expected, the busier town centre section will have less to see compared to some of the wilder sections away from the town.

Food stops

There are loads of options around Bedford town centre, including country pubs, bars, restaurants and cafés. Riverside spots, such as the Danish Camp, are a favourite: https://danishcamp.co.uk/.

Other activities

There is plenty on offer within Bedford, with the remains of a castle, museums, country parks, markets and even river festivals to explore. Why not support The John Bunyan Community Boat, which offers a range of scenic river cruises along the River Great Ouse from April to October. The boat is operated on behalf of the Bedford & Milton Keynes Waterway Trust. All funds and donations raised go towards the development of a new 26km waterway park, which will link the River Great Ouse in Bedford to the Grand Union Canal in Milton Keynes. The boat is run entirely by volunteers and is open to everyone.

NEED TO KNOW

- A Waterways Licence is required for this stretch of water (see page 12 for more information). Paddle UK offers good value membership, which includes access to the water, third party public liability insurance and various discounts nationwide.

- The Top River section of this paddle can get extremely busy. Exercise caution and adhere to the keep to the right rule of paddling.

RIGHT Top River.

29 CARDINGTON TO BEDFORD TOWN CENTRE

The Great Ouse is a heavyweight among English rivers, clocking in at around 225–257km long! It starts its journey in Northamptonshire, winds its way through several counties and finally empties into the North Sea near King's Lynn. The Great Ouse is a river that can cater for all abilities, with faster flowing stretches for the more experienced, to slower, wider sections for all to enjoy. You'll experience nature at its finest in some of the wilder sections, or why not try an urban paddle through the town centre. Cardington is a small village located in the Borough of Bedford, Bedfordshire. It is best known for its historical ties to the aviation industry, particularly during World War I.

The Lowdown

DISTANCE 3.8km
WATER TYPE River
DIFFICULTY ●
LICENCE REQUIRED ✓ (see Need to know box)

PARKING Priory Business Park Stannard Way, Cardington, Bedford MK44 3SG, ///stamp.smoke.circle. Small, free unnamed car park off Stannard Way. Follow signs towards the Cardington Slalom course.

LAUNCH POINT ///kicked.follow.filer. To access the water, carry your kit and head over the weir bridge towards Priory Park (above). Follow the path a short way until you reach the designated portage points on the left, which will be heading upstream on the river.

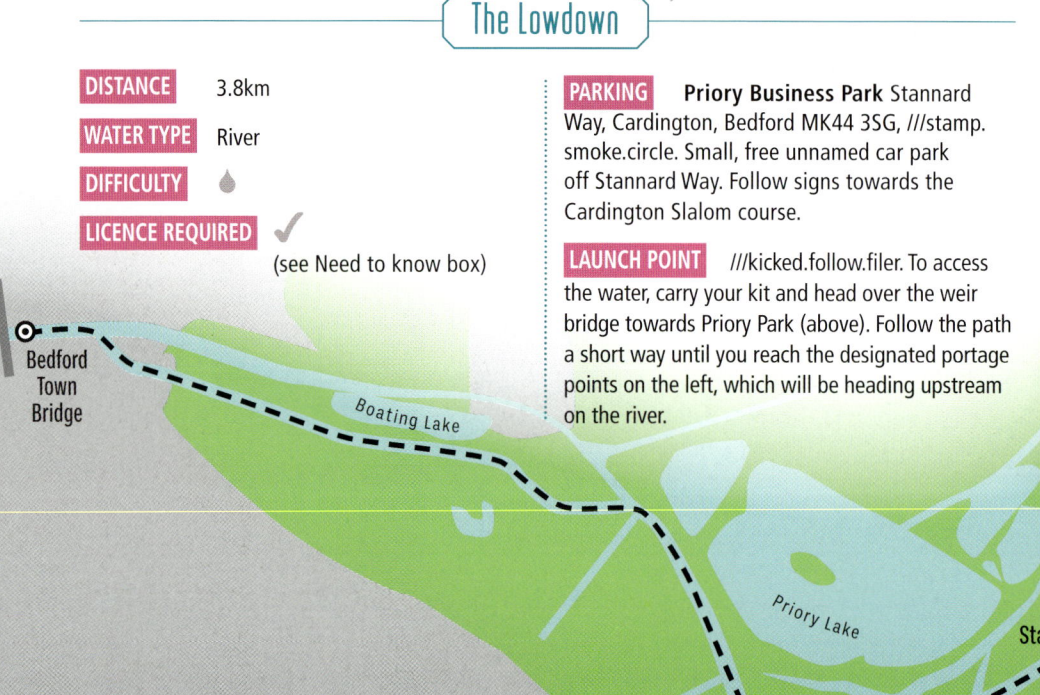

ABOVE Paddling past the Oasis Beach public swimming pool

History

Bedford is a historic market town on the River Great Ouse, situated on the arc between Oxford and Cambridge. It began life as a Saxon village, due to its location as an excellent river crossing point.

The river cuts through the Fens, a historically marshy region. Over time, clever engineering projects have been put in place to drain the land using the Ouse, making it more farmable. Over the centuries, Bedford became an important market town. Vikings raided it, but the English fought back and built a castle (which is mostly gone now). Bedford used to be famous for making wool and lace, but today it has a mixture of businesses. The town still has a lovely old centre with some reminders of its history, like a big church and a castle mound.

The paddle

When you launch, be mindful of the locks and boom before the weir – you will be paddling in the opposite direction to these to head towards Bedford town centre. Paddle upstream, and you'll see the water inlet for the Cardington Canoe Slalom Course, the first humanmade white-water course in the country. Events are held here throughout the year. Carry on past and on your left you'll see the Kingfisher hotel, which offers a nice waterside patio where you can stop for a break and refreshments should you wish.

Carry on straight for a while now, and you'll see a row of moored boats before the river bends towards the right. Be mindful of moving traffic here. You'll carry on past the entrance of Priory Marina, where various narrowboats and houseboats are moored. From here follow the main river to the left, meandering through the trees. In the distance you might spot a strange pyramid shape that looks totally out of place – this is the Oasis Beach public swimming pool. Shortly after, you'll paddle under three bridges, one of which is the disused Bedford to Sandy train line, which is now part of the National Cycle Route 51.

Continue paddling, and on the right you'll see Longholme Boating Lake. Keep left of the 'island' and carry on straight – this is where you'll enter 'Bottom River', which ends at Duck Mill/Abbey Bridge, where you'll see a slalom course set up by the Viking Canoe Club and later renamed the Etienne Stott Arena after the Olympian canoeist Etienne Stott, who trained in Bedford and won gold in the C2 canoe slalom at the London 2012 Summer Olympics.

If you wish to portage earlier, there are two options on your right, just by Schools' Boathouse. The best option is to stick close to the building, and walk north towards what is known as 'Top River' (see Kempston to Bedford town centre & Top River, page 162) – you will see a concrete jetty ahead where you can access the water. Carry on left and you'll be in the centre of Bedford.

For recommendations on Wildlife, Food stops and Other activities, please refer to these sections in the Kempston to Bedford town centre & Top River paddle, on page 162.

> **NEED TO KNOW**
>
> ■ A Waterways Licence is required for this stretch of water (see page 12 for more information). Paddle UK offers good value membership, which includes access to the water, third party public liability insurance and various discounts nationwide.

TOP RIGHT Etienne Stott Arena.
RIGHT Slalom Course at the Etienne Stott Arena.
BELOW Calm day for a paddle in Cardington.

CARDINGTON TO BEDFORD TOWN CENTRE

The Etienne Stott White Water Arena
In recognition of Etienne Stott's Gold Medal Winning Performance at the London 2012 Olympic Games
BEDFORD BOROUGH COUNCIL

30 GREAT BARFORD TO WILLINGTON LOCK

The Great Ouse is a heavyweight among English rivers, clocking in at around 225–257km long! It starts its journey in Northamptonshire, winds its way through several counties and finally empties into the North Sea near King's Lynn. The Great Ouse is a river that can cater for all abilities, with faster flowing stretches for the more experienced, to slower, wider sections for all to enjoy. You'll experience nature at its finest in some of the wilder sections, or why not try an urban paddle through the town centre.

The Lowdown

DISTANCE 2km
WATER TYPE River
DIFFICULTY ●
LICENCE REQUIRED ✓ (see Need to know box)
PARKING New Road, Great Barford MK44 3HW, ///essays.gliders.meanders. Free on-road parking next to the Anchor Inn. Please check local road signage.
LAUNCH POINT ///bucket.steam.judges. Launch from the public green across the road.

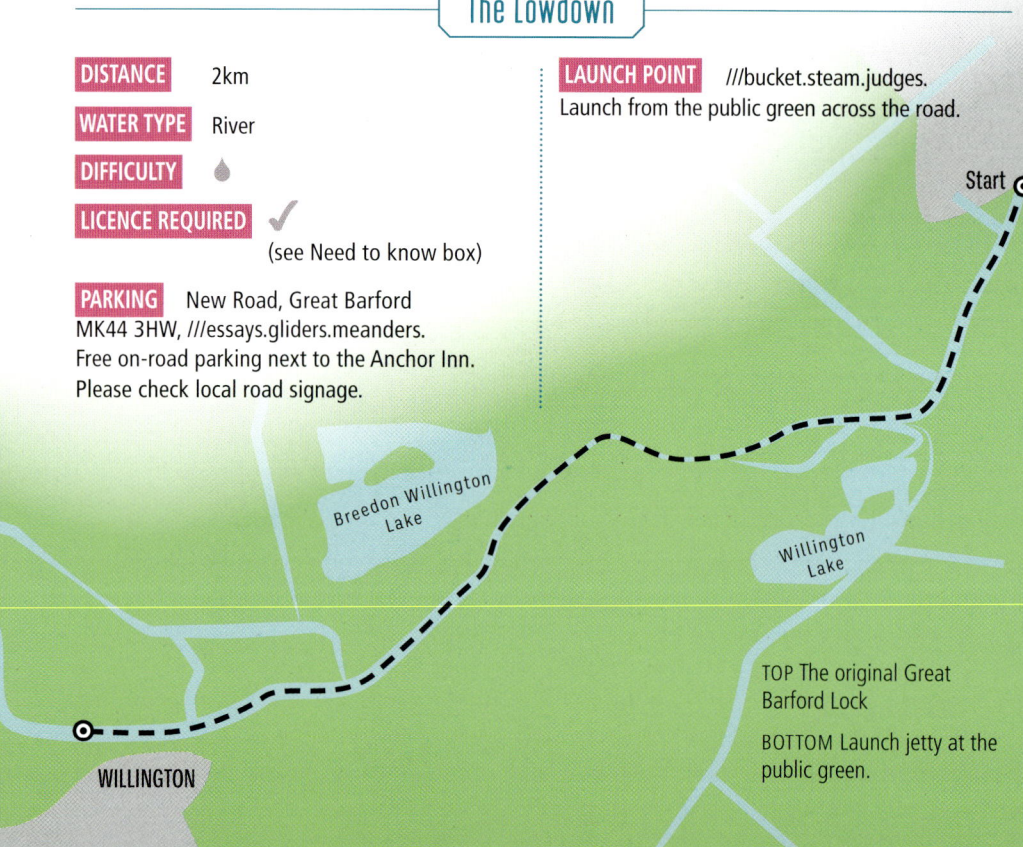

TOP The original Great Barford Lock

BOTTOM Launch jetty at the public green.

History

Great Barford is a charming village nestled in Bedfordshire, England. Its history dates back centuries, with evidence of settlement dating to the Anglo-Saxon period. Great Barford prospered during the medieval period, likely due to its location on the River Great Ouse, which provided a vital transportation route. The village's iconic All Saints Church, with its 15th-century tower, is a testament to its rich history. In the past, the village was home to Great Barford Castle, a Norman motte and bailey castle. During the Industrial Revolution, Great Barford experienced growth as a result of various industries, including agriculture and manufacturing.

Today, Great Barford retains its historic charm while offering a modern lifestyle. Its beautiful surroundings, rich history, and friendly community make it a desirable place to live and visit.

The paddle

Launching from the public green (page 173, bottom), head right upstream, paddling under the road bridge. You'll meander through lots of countryside on this short paddle. When you arrive at Willington Lock, please be mindful of the weir. You can turn back here for a short paddle, or you can portage here and carry on towards Danish Camp (https://

danishcamp.co.uk/), a riverside café that often runs special events throughout the year. This adds just under 1km to your paddle.

For longer paddles, you can extend your trip upstream towards Cardington (see Cardington to Bedford town centre, page 168).

For recommendations on Wildlife, Food stops and Other activities, please refer to these sections in the Kempston to Bedford town centre & Top River paddle, on page 162.

BELOW Picturesque Great Barford Bridge.

NEED TO KNOW

■ A Waterways Licence is required for this stretch of water (see page 12 for more information). Paddle UK offers good value membership, which includes access to the water, third party public liability insurance and various discounts nationwide.

■ Be mindful of the road and moving traffic when parking and carrying kit.

GREAT BARFORD TO WILLINGTON LOCK

BELOW Aerial shot of Great Barford Bridge.

HERTFORDSHIRE

Hertfordshire, often referred to as Herts, is a historic and picturesque county in the southeast of England, located just north of London. Known for its rolling countryside, charming villages and rich history, Hertfordshire seamlessly blends rural tranquillity with urban accessibility. The county boasts a diverse landscape from serene rivers to beautiful nature reserves, and there is ample opportunities for outdoor activities such as hiking, cycling and, most importantly paddling!

Hertfordshire's history stretches back to Roman times, evident in sites like the ruins of Verulamium in St Albans, which also features a stunning cathedral and a vibrant market town atmosphere. The county played a significant role during the medieval period, with numerous castles, manor houses and historic churches dotting the landscape. Notable landmarks include the stately Hatfield House, a prime example of Jacobean architecture, and the enchanting Knebworth House, known for its beautiful gardens and rock concerts.

The county's excellent transport links, including major motorways and rail services, provide easy access to London and other parts of the UK, making it an ideal location for both commuters and tourists.

With its rich heritage, scenic beauty and vibrant communities, Hertfordshire offers a unique blend of the old and the new, making it a captivating destination for residents and visitors alike.

TOP Poppy the dog enjoying a scenic paddle on a sunny day on the River Stort.

RIGHT River reeds on a frosty morning on the River Stort.

31 BISHOP'S STORTFORD TO TWYFORD MILL LOCK

The River Stort meanders for 38km from just south of Langley village to Feildes Weir in Hoddesdon, at the confluence of the River Lea and River Stort. This is a beautiful landscape of water mills and nature reserves. The railway line runs parallel with the river, so you can paddle the length of the Stort and get the train back to your starting point. There is so much history and wildlife to be seen here, and with Bishop's Stortford surrounding either side of the river, it is a very sheltered spot. It does open up closer to Twyford Mill Lock, with fields either side, making for a beautiful backdrop. Therefore you have best of both worlds on this paddle: a historic town brimming with fascinating history and architecture, and beautiful countryside with nature reserves running alongside allowing you to see some wonderful wildlife along the way.

The Lowdown

DISTANCE 5–10km

WATER TYPE River

DIFFICULTY

LICENCE REQUIRED
(see Need to know box)

PARKING Thorley Street Pig Lane, Bishop's Stortford: CM22 7PA, ///worth.patrol.amount. At Twyford Mill Lock. Free at time of writing. Plenty of spaces available.

LAUNCH POINT  Twyford Mill Lock ///worth.patrol.amount
Bishop's Stortford ///flying.causes.slap

History

The River Stort Navigation is split into three branches. The head of the navigation in Bishop's Stortford is called Hockerill Cut, while the two other branches are Terminus Basin and Mill Stream. In its heyday, this stretch of the canal was busy with dockyards and working boats plying their trade to London. But these days you'll see the canal boats moored up as pleasure craft.

On this stretch of river, you'll notice The Maltings, with their unusual chimneys, the oldest part of which dates back to 1843. Malthouses converted barley grain to malt for brewing beer. Stortford had a large brewery but the malt was mostly shipped to brewers in London.

The locks were built specifically to fit only the Stort barges, meaning the River Lea barges couldn't use them!

BISHOP'S STORTFORD TO TWYFORD MILL LOCK

The paddle
Paddling from Twyford Mill Lock towards Bishop's Stortford equates to 5km one way, making this a 10km paddle if you wish to do a return journey. For the one-way paddle, you'll need to organise a shuttle by leaving a car at either end (see above for car parking information).

The nearest car park to the launch point in Bishop's Stortford is the Sainsbury's multi-storey car park, which does have a height barrier and is a pay and display car park. This also means navigating paddlecraft around a multi-storey, but if you have an inflatable craft, you could deflate at the portage point and carry it across the road to the car park.

From Thorley Street car park, exit to the left and cross over the bridge. To the left straight after the bridge is the portage point to enter the river. Enter the river and go right towards Bishop Stortford.

As you paddle, you'll enter Rushy Mead Nature Reserve, formerly a sewage pumping station and now a lush wetland habitat for marsh marigolds, dragonflies, damselflies and water beetles.

Continuing on to the one portage point on this paddle at South Mill Lock. Exit on the right and walk past the lock to enter the river again towards South Mill.

As you approach Bishop's Stortford you'll pass the Millennium Bridge, The Maltings, the Waterside Stortford mural, after which you'll enter the town, where this paddle ends, as the stretch of water further up is not accessible to paddlers. You'll see a J.D. Wetherspoon's to the left, and there is gap here which you can paddle to and portage.

Wildlife
The River Stort is surrounded by RSPB nature reserves and there is plenty of wildlife to be seen, including mallards, moorhens, kingfisher, grey wagtails, herons, blackcap, house martins, pied wagtails, starlings, coots, great spotted woodpeckers, goldfinch, mute swans,

swallows, sparrowhawks and many more. Other species include otters, water voles, pipistrelle bats, butterflies, damselflies and moths.

Food stops

There are multiple food stops in the town of Bishop's Stortford. There is also a portage point/landing stage at J.D. Wetherspoon's, where you can stop off and enjoy refreshments.

Other activities

Bishop's Stortford is a busy town and there is plenty to do here. The Bishop's Stortford Museum has local history, themed walks and talks, and lots of activities for the kids (especially during the holidays): https://southmillarts.co.uk/stortford-museum. There's also several Escape Rooms, shopping centres, and local farms and farm shops in the surrounding areas.

NEED TO KNOW

- A Waterways Licence is required for this stretch of water (see page 12 for more information). Paddle UK offers good value membership, which includes access to the water, third party public liability insurance and various discounts nationwide.
- This stretch of the river is used by pleasure craft, so take care and observe the keep right rule for paddling.

RIGHT An autumnal paddle on the River Stort near Twyford Lock.

BISHOP'S STORTFORD TO TWYFORD MILL LOCK 185

RIGHT Canal boats on the River Stort.
BELOW Canal boats by the Nature Reserve.

BOTTOM (left to right) Andy, Jess, Oli and Matt on a cold Strood paddle.

TOP A rainbow of kayaks at Pin Mill.

OVERLEAF EOEPs circumnavigation around Mersea SUP challenge.

PHOTO CREDITS

Andy Large 48, 69, 70, 98, 123, 125, 135, 136, 137, 138, 139, 141, 143, 144, 145, 147, 148, 149, 150, 151, 153
Barry Scott 188–89
Anthony Cullen Photography 94–5
Claire King 68
Clare Hammond 39 (bottom), 40 (bottom)
Colm O'Laoi 17 (bottom), 18, 20, 31, 33, 42, 43, 100
Elaine Wilson 154–55, 156
Hannah Johns 101
Helen Dobie 38, 39 (top), 179, 182
James Crisp 51, 64 (top)
Jason Botelho 114–115
Jess Ashley 6, 15, 19, 22 (bottom), 24, 32, 34, 35, 64 (bottom), 66, 96, 120
Jon Hipkin 27, 75 (top)
Lian Smith-Simmonds 157, 184 (left)
Lucy Small 173 (top)
Marcin Mioducki 161, 165–66, 176–77
Matt Gardner 91
Matt Payne 46–7, 104, 105, 106, 107, 116, 117, 119, 121, 128–29, 130–31, 132–33
Michael Dean 158
Miriam Kopacova 29
Paul Holmes 166–67, 170
Paul Thwaites 54, 55
Petra Studholme 37, 40 (top), 164–65, 178, 185
Oli Jordan 14, 56, 61, 63, 65, 74 (top), 75 (bottom), 77 (bottom), 79, 82, 83, 85, 86, 87, 88, 103, 159, 160, 171, 173 (bottom), 174–75
Oli Jordan and **Andy Large** 7, 8, 9
Rachel Bedford 110, 111, 113
Richard Hedges 58, 59, 89
Rich Wright 97
Sarah Du Plessis 78
Shaun Mills 80–1
Stephen Huntley 186, 187
Stuart Koenig-Roach 77 (top)
Tom Fall 22 (top)
Tom Payne 25
Tony Bryant 109
Tracy Edwards 127

INDEX

A

Alresford Creek 18
Anglian Water Ways 13
Alresford 49

B

Bargate 134–7
Beccles 142
Bedford 162–6, 168–70, 175
Beeleigh Falls 64
Beeleigh Lock 24
Bird's Dyke 135
Bishop's Stortford 38, 180–2
Black Sluice Navigation 13
Blackwater Estuary 50, 51, 52, 57, 62, 64, 70, 71, 76
Blackwater Navigation 21–5
Bottom River, Great Ouse 170
Brightlingsea 16–20, 30, 31, 33–4, 49
    Estuary and Creeks 30–4
Broads National Park 13, 117–43
Brundall 134, 136
Bull Meadow 47
Bungay Loop 140–2
Bunney's Broad 135
Bures 98–101
Buxton Mill 118–21

C

Cambridge 13, 144, 152–8
Cambridgeshire Fens 148
Cardington 168–70, 175
Cattawade 42–3
Chelmer & Blackwater Navigation 21–5, 62, 63, 64
Chelmsford 14, 21, 23, 24–5
Colchester 13, 14, 48–9
Colne Estuary 16, 17–18, 31–2, 45, 49, 57, 60, 71, 74, 76
Coltishall 118–21
Crouch Estuary 12

D

Dedham 12, 41–3
Ditchingham 142
Dovercourt Bay 26–9
Doyle Dam 112

E

East Mersea 31, 58, 72, 77
Ely 146–50

F

Flag Creek 32
Flatford 41–3
Fleet Dyke 126, 135–6

G

Goldhanger Creek 52
Great Barford 172–5
Great Henny 99, 101

H

Harlow 36–40
Harwich 28, 88–9
Heybridge 21–5
    Basin 24–5, 62, 64
Horstead Mill 120
Hythe 18, 45, 49

I

Ipswich 94

K

Kempston 162–6, 170, 175

L

Lamarsh 98–101
Langham 112
Langham Flumes 108–13
Littleport 148

INDEX

M
Maldon 25
  Loop 62–6
Mersea Island 57–61, 71–5
  Circumnavigation 76–9
Mersea Strood 16, 31, 58, 71–5
Mettingham 142
Mulberry Harbour 53–6, 67–70

N
Nayland 102–4
Newman's Hole 135
Norfolk Broads 13, 117–43
Norwich 128–33

O
Osea Island 50–2

P
Packing Shed Island 72
Papermill Lock 22, 23–4
Pin Mill 93–7
Pitmire Weir 99
Point Clear Bay 31, 32
Point Clear Lagoon 32
Pyefleet Creek 16, 17, 31

R
Ray Creek 31–2
River Ancholme 13
River Blackwater 50, 51, 52, 58, 62, 64
River Bure 119
River Cam 13, 153–8
River Chelmer 13, 51, 62, 64
River Colne 13, 34, 45–9
River Crouch 14
River Deben 84, 86
River Gipping 93, 96
River Glen 13
River Great Ouse 13, 146–50, 160–75
River Nene 13
River Orwell 93–7
River Stort 38, 40, 180–2
River Stour 13, 36, 42–4, 92, 93, 98–101, 108, 111, 113
River Thames 14, 53
River Waveney 140–2

River Welland 13
River Wensum 128, 129, 132
River Yare 126, 129, 134–5
Rockland Broad 124–6, 135, 137
Rockland Dyke 135
Rockland Staithe 126, 134, 137
Rowhedge 16, 48, 49
Rushy Mead Nature Reserve 181

S
Saffron Waldon 14
St John Ilketshall 142
St Osyth Creek 31–2
Sawbridgeworth 36–40
Shalford Weir 99
Short Dykes 126
Slaughter, the rearrange 124–6
Southend-on-Sea 14, 70
  Pier 55, 67–70
Springfield Basin 21, 22, 23
Stratford St Mary 43, 108–13
Sudbury 90–2
Surlingham 134
  Broad 134–7
  Fleet 135, 136

T
Thames Estuary 53, 67
Tollesbury 57–61
Top River, Great Ouse 162–6, 170, 175
Town Hard 20, 34
Two Tree Island 53–6
Twyford Mill Lock 180–2

W
Waldringfield 84–9
West Mersea 58, 72, 77
Wilford Bridge 85–6
Willington Lock 172–5
Wissington Weir 102–4
Wiston 103
Wivenhoe 16–20, 31, 48, 49
Woodbridge 88
Wroxham 121

ACKNOWLEDGEMENTS

Firstly, we would like to thank Bloomsbury for giving us the opportunity to write our first book and become authors! It's been an experience we will never forget, and we are so proud of our achievements.

We would all like to thank those nearest and dearest to us who have put up with us and supported us throughout this whole process.

Oli I would like to thank my parents, Karen and Richard Jordan, for letting me move back and take over, whilst building East of England Paddlesports, to Andy Large, Nick Devenney, Hannah Johns, Jessica Ashley, Matt Payne, Richard Wright and Jason Botelho – all of whom have given up time to help run the group and shape it to what it is today! Thanks to Rich Wright and Natasha Sonnes, who helped with some wording for Suffolk, Paul Thwaites for the history of Mulberry Harbour and Ashley Heritage for helping with Bedford! And, lastly, thanks to everyone who's joined the group, joined us for a paddle, bought some club merch or offered advice, the group wouldn't be the same without you!

Andy When I started paddling for leisure after retiring from a long corporate career, little did I know what it would lead to. A year later, in 2019, I met Oli and was asked to help run East of England Paddlesports. This started the journey to writing this book with lots of adventures along the way, and hopefully many more to come. Huge thanks to Oli for taking that first step with me and to all the lovely people who I have met along the way – those I've paddled with, laughed and cried with, and camped and travelled with. I have met and made lifelong friends here – people I know I can count on and who care for me – all down to the power of the paddle! Above all, I would like to thank my wife, Liz – without without her help and support, none of this would be possible.

Jess I would like to thank my husband, Joe, and my son, Noah, for supporting me through it all – being taken to various places to explore, paddle and be asked to take a million photos, and for understanding all those early hours, late nights and long days away from home to research for this book. A big thank you to Clare Hammond for the words and photos for Sawbridgeworth, Petra Studholme for taking me to Bishop's Stortford. Despite the torrential downpour making it unsafe to paddle, we still had a lovely (but very wet) walk of the whole paddle route! Thanks to Colm O'Laoi for supplying us with so many wonderful eye-catching aerial photos of various destinations of the East coast. And last but not least, thank you to Oli, Andy and Matt. Without you guys I would not have been able to complete this task of writing a book, and to say I have done it with my mates is the best feeling ever! Who would have thought joining a Paddlesports group would then lead to all these amazing opportunities and, best of all, making some lifelong friends and some wonderful memories along the way!

Matt When Oli came to us and said, "We've been asked to write a book", my initial thoughts were "You're crazy", especially when I have a newborn child. But here we are – we've done it! But I wouldn't have been able to achieve it without the incredible support from my family, friends and, of course, our East of England Paddlesports members. Firstly, Abbie and George, thank you so much for supporting me to be able to spend days and weekends away from home to paddle some of the beautiful places around the East coast doing the sport I love. I would like to thank Duncan Wyer for providing history and advice for the Norwich City and Norfolk Broad paddles. I wouldn't have known where to start without you. And, finally, thank you Oli, Jess and Andy for inviting and accepting me into this incredible community.

We would all like to thank those who have been credited on page 187 for all the wonderful photos sent to us, so that we can showcase East Anglia at its finest! We are truly humbled by all the help and support we have received from all those around us, from family, friends to all the group members from East of England Paddlesports! Thank you!

PRAISE FOR JESSE Q. SUTANTO

Dial A for Aunties

"Sutanto brilliantly infuses comedy and culture into the unpredictable rom-com/murder mystery mashup." —*USA Today* (four-star review)

"It's a high-wire act of comic timing, misunderstandings, romantic foibles and possibly foiled heists." —*The New York Times Book Review*

"If you loved *Crazy Rich Asians* and all the comedic family drama, you'll definitely get a kick out of this story." —*PopSugar*

"Part thriller, part rom-com, Jesse Q. Sutanto's *Dial A for Aunties* will give you the good laugh we could all use these days." —*Marie Claire*

"Wrap a rom-com with a crime novel, sprinkle in *Weekend at Bernie's*, and you get this deliciously fun, big-hearted book." —*BookRiot*

"*Dial A for Aunties* has redefined what 'page-turner' means to me.... If you're in the mood for laugh-out-loud humor, unprecedented mayhem (involving meddlesome family members and over-the-top drama), and delightful twists and turns at every corner, I highly recommend *Dial A for Aunties*." —*BuzzFeed*

"A delicious and devourable read." —*E! Online*

The Obsession

"A suspenseful page-turner." —*Kirkus Reviews*

"This tense, quick-moving thriller is also a thought-provoking story about the different shapes of abuse. Fans of high-drama fiction with a dark edge, like Karen McManus's *One of Us Is Lying*, will be hooked."
—*School Library Journal*

Books by Jesse Q. Sutanto

For Adults

Dial A for Aunties

Four Aunties and a Wedding

For Young Adults

The Obsession

The New Girl